BASIC BOOKS IN EDUCATION

Editor: *Kathleen O'Connor, B.Sc., Senior*
Lecturer in Education, Rolle College, Exmouth
Advisory Editor: *D. J. O'Connor, M.A., Ph.D.*
Professor of Philosophy, University of Exeter

SCHOOLING IN THE MIDDLE YEARS –
Art for Children

This book gives students and less experienced teachers a brief introduction to some of the theory and practice of art teaching, with special reference to the eight-to-twelve age group. There is information about materials and processes, together with lists of addresses of suppliers.

Most of the chapters have both theoretical and practical components. The theory is simple and necessarily brief, designed to provide a series of links between art teaching and basic educational thinking. The many practical starting points and ideas offer suggestions for initiating and guiding art-orientated work in schools, with the aim of inducing conditions where children may gain the opportunity and confidence to be purposefully active and creative.

Key words in the text are in SMALL CAPITALS, there are summaries and 'further reading' lists at the end of most chapters and there is a full bibliography, glossary and index.

SCHOOLING IN THE MIDDLE YEARS—

Art for Children

MICHAEL HOYLAND

MACMILLAN

First published 1970 by
MACMILLAN AND CO LTD
London and Basingstoke
Associated companies in New York Toronto
Dublin Melbourne Johannesburg and Madras

SBN (boards) 333 05242 0
(paper) 333 10252 5

Printed in Great Britain by
ROBERT MACLEHOSE AND CO LTD
The University Press, Glasgow

Contents

Contents

List of Illustrations

Preface

All the children in a school benefit when art activities are a natural and lasting part of school life; for well-taught art brings an inventive sense of purpose to children, and self-respect. Sometimes, through art, a good teacher can waken something in a child that will open up new worlds for him, and change his life. And to be a good teacher of art you do not need to be a skilled specialist.

This book is written for students who are looking for a brief introduction to art teaching that gives particular attention to children between eight and twelve: the very important period in the life of a child covered by the expression 'the middle years of schooling'. Most of the book is also written for practising teachers.

Throughout, I have used the word 'art' to cover any activity in schools that can be thought of as lying within the traditional boundaries of 'Art and Crafts'.

M.H.

Acknowledgement

I wish to thank all the children and adults who have influenced this book.

1 Reasons

If undertakings are to be successful, it is necessary to believe in them; and in order to believe in the value of any undertaking, it is necessary to know why it is valuable. This chapter, which is more theoretical than the other chapters, will touch on some of the major and minor reasons that lie behind the immense undertaking of art education. Once the necessary theory has been outlined, we can begin to think about relating it to art activities in school.

The more important reasons that cause us to undertake whatever we do are often the most difficult to put convincingly, because they involve subjective judgements of values and usually carry wide implications. For example, precise reasons for the choice of a profession or a house are often difficult to find; and the motives behind the choice of a husband or wife can be impenetrable. If we look at art education and ask 'Why?', certain answers suggest themselves that have great power; but they cannot be exactly proved.

All through history there has been conflict between the free and enquiring spirit of man, which resents constraint, and the other – narrower – spirit that not only seeks security for itself in conformism, but also works to impose it on others. For many years, sensitive people have been aware of a crisis in society that seems to be connected with the growth of industrialisation. There are 'things about' modern society that have profoundly troubled such perceptive writers and artists as Kafka (40),* Aldous Huxley (37), Munch, and Francis Bacon. When we examine what these and many others have said in their work, in varied ways, it seems that individual integrity, and freedom of thought and action, are

* Numbers in parentheses refer to Bibliography, pages 120-122 ff.

being seriously threatened by modern pressures. In simple terms, a significant part of what we are being warned against is *conformism*.

Connected with this danger is the *compartmentalism* that afflicts many organisations today. Society is producing more and more people who are highly skilled in a small area of knowledge and activity, but so narrow in outlook that they are as unwilling to move about in what they consider other people's preserves as they are to cross from their own front gardens into their neighbours'. It is not only our houses that suggest rows of boxes.

Mental rigidity and narrowness can be countered by independent and comprehensive thinking, and an important part of the responsibility for encouraging the free processes of thought rests on anyone concerned with education. It is not enough to prepare people for society nowadays; instead, we need to prepare better people for a better society: people who are flexible and wise enough to adapt themselves to an unsatisfactory society while they are themselves changing it for the better.

In order to be what they are, creative artists need to be able to respond and think independently; and this is why the artist, in the broadest sense, stands to lose so much from conformist and hackneyed habits of mind. His thinking and working have to be thoroughly flexible, and unaffected by academic barriers, if he is to make a contribution to his art. It follows that to any system of education seeking to nourish and sustain originality and freedom of spirit, the artist's outlook and methods have much to offer. Children who are encouraged to respond and think formatively for themselves, as artists do, and who use the methods of artists to explore the world, are not likely to fall an easy prey to rigid or narrow habits of thought.

The truth of this has been recognised for a long time, and art has gained increasing importance in schools. Yet we have far to go; there are still many schools where art, and all that it represents, are barely touched on.

DRIVES AND NEEDS

Alongside the broad reasons for art education there are more intimate reasons. Of these, one of the most persuasive is this: art is closely involved with *the desire to explore* – which it can express, satisfy or increase.

Everyone is curious about something, but children of middle-school age are probably more curious about anything new to them than anyone else. In fact, many want to know so much that adults become exasperated. But adults should try to be patient; for the wish to search and find out is a vital force in a child's learning. If he had no curiosity at all, no spirit of adventure, a child would learn very little.[1]*

Children search with curiosity not only in order to find out about the nature of things – their 'thingness' – but also to discover where they themselves stand in relation to things. It is possible that a young child sees the chair that he sits on as being part of himself, and the search for disentanglement and comprehensible groupings around the self continues into adolescence. (As regards your own self, are you always sure how you stand in relation to the objects marked on a map?) Children experience life with less intervention by thought than adults do, which means that sight and touch have exceptional and vivid significance for them. And these experiences coming through their eyes and fingers are used to explain and disentangle. This is partly why drawing, painting and making things are important. A child's clay model of a bus will teach him more about the nature of buses.[2]

In many kinds of play there are elements of exploration. Like dreams and art, play brings experiences together and obliquely explains them. Even though a child may appear to be playing without purpose, or the things he makes while he plays are not finished by adult standards, it may well be that the very activity of playing or making helps him to see better how he is himself related to particular objects or people. A drawing of his mother will often bring better understanding not only of the mother but also of how he stands in relation to her – of how each feels towards the other. Read saw play as a form of art in itself, an expression of the child's relation to life.[3]

From the teacher's point of view, it is the creative kind of exploring that is the most valuable. Creative exploration can either be individual or co-operative, and it has a three-fold character:

* Small numbers refer to notes at the end of the chapter.

enquiry leading to making, which leads to explanation and understanding. That is to say, in brief: *explore – make – understand*.

It should not be forgotten that being creative is not always a pleasant experience. Some adult artists and writers suffer acutely in their work. Nevertheless, anyone who makes something he feels to be worthwhile at the time of making it will gain self respect; and this holds great significance for children, especially for those who are unsure of themselves. Moreover, through feeling pleased with their work at first, and then being critical or even contemptuous about it later on, children (as well as adults) develop a scale of values.

The desire to make things is strong and ancient; without it, man would not have conquered nature. The act of forming something out of a plastic material with one's own hands, until a visible and touchable object comes into being, which is in some way an extension of one's thoughts, seems – for a while – to lay some innate ghost. It gives a sense of power over lifeless material, which brings a little security. Perhaps we are all not quite sure of the material world in certain ways (how much trust can we really put in *things*?) and this is the kind of reassurance we need. Our ARTEFACTS are thoughts made visible: frozen thoughts. So long as they are not too imperfect we draw courage from them.

There are some interesting similarities and important links between creative activity and dreaming. MacKenzie shows how, in dreams, it appears as if our minds were constantly trying to organise their experiences into forms meaningful enough to allow us to feel and behave coherently.[4] Some theorists think that dreams are both reflections of the ways in which our minds attempt to formulate the conflicts and problems of our lives, and one of the means by which we unconsciously try to solve them. In short, that dreams both formulate and solve.

Art, too, is concerned with posing problems and solving them. Artistic activities, having deep connections with the unconscious mind, help to integrate its unwordly evolutions with the processes of the conscious mind, and so also with the outside world. In some senses, art is an extension of our dreams into consciousness: a form of wakeful and problem-solving dreaming.

The relationship becomes clearer when one considers that dreams are mainly visual and pictorial, and they are charged with emotion.[5] In a dream, reality is grasped at through emotion very much as it is in a work of art. Furthermore, dreaming has its wishful sides, and so has art: both seek at times to make knowable a wished-for state of affairs. A potter who tries again and again to make a completely satisfying form is trying to make a reality out of an ideal.

When someone is day-dreaming, he builds fantasies that are not only coloured with emotion, as in night-dreaming, but also with the processes of his conscious imagination. Day-dreams lead naturally into works of art; an artist's coming-to-terms emotionally with a piece of work that he is doing is often a form of realistic, or plastic, day-dreaming. Imagination is a powerful unifying function.[6] It brings together thought-images and feeling-images into varied relationships, and it becomes stronger from stimulation and use. Unfortunately, it is only rarely, at present, that children in school are able to follow up the day-dreams that arise from a story, a description, or some new experience, by going off alone and producing a new work of art.

Further understanding of the importance of art in human development can come from a study of the probable drives behind prehistoric art. Although a great deal remains conjecture, it seems likely that many prehistoric artefacts were the expression of an ancient metaphysical and mythical system of ideas, in which all kinds of needs were satisfied. Some cave pictures may have been painted as back-cloths to rites or 'theatre'. There was probably an aesthetic, as well as a profane element; sometimes children went into the caves and made their own childish contributions, either under the direction of early Palaeolithic art teachers, or casually

(80). In our individual and personal development, drawing came before writing; and so it was with mankind.

It is well known that symbolism and magic played a part in the dark and disturbing interiors of the caves; and even now, in our modern un-superstitious society, art retains symbolic and even magical meanings. (Many of our technological achievements are magic come to life.) To a child, there is still a breath of magic in the reduction of a heavy and obviously solid lorry into flat shapes on a small piece of paper, or the transformation of a human figure into a lump of clay. With regard to symbolism, almost any shape or colour has symbolic associations.

It has been said that children are creatures of feeling first, imagination second, and intellect third. (If you are a student, you might interpret this in the light of your study of child development.) When used properly in a school, art activities appeal naturally to the emotional life of the children, bringing it together in a constantly varying interaction with the lives of their imaginations and intellects. This is how completeness is reached: children can become involved 'heart and soul' with what they do.

In any school where feeling has begun to lead freely into expression, special links of communication are formed between individuals; and in such a school, few children are unable to say something worthwhile in some medium.

As experienced teachers know, children express many drives that conflict with society's customs, and often with the children's own interests. These negative tendencies have to be met, as far as possible, with intelligent tolerance; but drives in which fear aggression is present must be resisted. A teacher can meet these drives by sensitively using art to work them out and redirect them into positive activities. For example, a child who fears water may learn to face up to it through 'painting out' his fear in a series of whirlpools and tidal waves.

By engaging minds, feelings and hands all at once, and by satisfying many emotional needs, art can permeate and enliven the life of a school.

Plate 1. *Balloon* 17″ × 30″. (Group work – 9 years.) A 'mosaic' made with squares cut from glossy magazines, and strips of newspaper. A strong buoyant shape.

Plate 2. *Civet Cat* 20″ × 30″. (Two girls – 12 years.) A delightfully ingenious and telling use of torn newspaper and black sugar paper.

WAYS OF SEEING

The retinal experience

There are probably as many ways of seeing as there are seeing eyes; and it is important for teachers to be aware of some of the issues raised by this diversity. The most obvious constituents of seeing are *the impressions, coming from outside, that are experienced on the retina of the eye*. These impressions are closely related to the 'working model' of the real world that a child develops inside himself in order to help him to understand it – and they are also what artists start with. The degree to which the original impressions are altered by an artist's personality as he works, determines the kind of artist he is, and the nature of his artefacts. A skilful painter or sculptor who copies retinal experiences with the minimum of alteration by his own personality may be said to produce a *perceptual* or *retinal* artefact, and he is usually referred to as being NATURALISTIC or highly *representational* in his work. (Clearly, other sense impressions, too, affect the nature of an artist's work, but there is no room here to pursue their implications.[7])

An artist who cannot interpret retinal impressions, who cannot add anything out of his own personality to what his eyes give him and to what he goes on to express, is one who sees unresponsively. Indeed, he can be said to *look* rather than *see*. The English painters of the pre-Raphaelite school were remarkably skilful, but sometimes they looked too hard.

The conceptual image

When an artist alters his experiences of the outer world with his feelings and thoughts, and by the movements of his fingers, into something concrete and different, he produces a personal and *conceptual* image, or artefact. Usually the experienced artist will not only be aware of the way his personality is affecting his work, but he will also give it rein. His likes and dislikes, and whatever he thinks important, will colour his work in a subtle series of processes that make it different from the outer world; and if it is successful, his work will possess new meaning for himself and other people. He will not be a naturalistic artist. Van Gogh's

B

sunflowers are a compelling conceptual vision; Constable's hay-wain is nearer to naturalism.

In order to understand better the breadth of artistic creativity, it is helpful to think of a progression in which almost purely retinal works of art lie at one end of a scale and almost purely conceptual (or abstract) works lie at the other. Nearly all the work of the major artists and sculptors lies between. The fashion, or artistic 'feel', of a period usually concentrates around some area on the scale; and this area, also, is almost always situated somewhere between the two extremes, having elements in it of both the abstract and the retinal. Mondrian and Ben Nichol-son come close to one extreme, Landseer and Frith to the other. Teachers need to be aware of the fashion of their time – but they also need to be cautious of it. The fashions of adults are altogether too narrow and authoritarian for the purposes of children.

There is reason to believe that most children of primary age prefer naturalistic pictures depicting familiar objects, and that this preference tends to reduce as the children grow older (73). It seems, too, that although children attempt representation of the outer world from an early age (73), their art is necessarily sym-bolic and SCHEMATIC up until a DEVELOPMENTAL AGE of about nine. To be a truly naturalistic painter or clay-modeller even an adult needs to be exceptionally clever, and however hard a child may try he will not produce a truly naturalistic piece of work. By reason of the limitation of his own hands and of his own childish understanding and personality, he will unavoidably make something that is to some extent unnaturalistic – which accounts for the fascinating variations in children's art.

Once they are more than nine-years-old in developmental age children usually become able to express retinal experiences less schematically than before, which is the beginning of a process that can eventually cause their art to grow less vital, although much closer to reality. A little later, at about eleven, they begin to develop the power to think abstractly; and this is when a good teacher begins to introduce the idea that it might be possible to extract the most important elements from certain objects and bring them together into new conceptual relationships. This analytical-imaginative process calls for no less observation than representational drawing, and more analysis. It is possible for children of this age to render down a real object into something so conceptual that it becomes abstract.

Strictly speaking, no piece of work is ever either purely retinal or abstract, because personality and hints of reality can never be wholly eliminated; and so it is best to think of *an abstract* as being any piece of work that holds no recognisable elements of the everyday world, and to think of *abstraction* as a process in which some conscious extracting from retinal experiences takes place. Work that is abstract, or relatively abstract, without having undergone abstraction, is better called *pattern*. Children enjoy making patterns from an early age, and pattern-making, with the later growth of logical ideas, remains a relevant approach towards abstraction (see pages 40-42).

Owing to present fashions, there is a danger today of attaching too much importance to the abstract side of art (see page 40), and this should be resisted. Usually the body of work in a truly creative school is concerned with reality in recognisable though conceptual forms, and truly abstract works are rare.

Unfortunately, the photograph and the detailed retinal painting still remain the yardsticks with which ill-educated people measure works of art. But children who are familiar with Egyptian sculpture, Byzantine mosaics or African masks are not likely to take this view. Furthermore, a teacher can help children to go on working formatively during the creatively barren years that come with logical thought, by varying the art environment and approach to suit individuals in such a way that art activities always remain fresh and exhilarating to them.

Of course, the work of both children and adults shows many characteristics besides the ones mentioned. Environment, temperament and perceptual qualities (for example, HAPTIC and VISUAL) all contribute to the making of different types of artist, many of which are interestingly discussed by Read in *Education Through Art* (64); although it is well to remember that his differentiations, like Lowenfeld's, are open to criticism.[8]

Because children's creative work must always be to some extent childishly conceptual, it forms a peculiarly non-adult world of its own: a *first-world*. It follows that, when looking at children's work, the sensitive teacher not only has to try to dissociate from personal likes and dislikes, but to cut off adult attitudes, too. He or she must step across the abyss and enter into the children's own territory. It is when this has been done that the teacher will best be able to help a child to grow, encouraging wisely with regard to materials and methods, in ways best suited to a particular personality and its stage of development. And all the time, the teacher must respect everything sincere that the child does, without trying to impose patterns of any kind. The child's growth is the teacher's central concern. The only right way of seeing and doing in art is the right one for the child at a particular stage; it is not the one that is right for the adult teacher.

Too often, children come to think they are unable to 'do art' because members of their family, or others, have said that they draw or paint badly. A teacher, through respecting a child's work, can lead the child gradually to respect it too, so that the child comes in turn to self-respect through that work; and this, probably more than anything else, will help balanced growth.

PURPOSES

Life and subjects

First there was life, and then there were Reading, Writing and Arithmetic. This sums up the tendency to compartmentalism that has plagued formal education probably since it began, and that is becoming an increasing problem throughout society. We are reaching a state of affairs where experts abound in every department of life, able to operate fully in only a very limited area, and although highly regarded in their own small sectors, virtually ignored elsewhere. It may not be long before every trained man is like a well: deep but narrow, and cut off from the world outside. Although compartmentalism and expertise clearly offer certain advantages, they cause difficulties even in the sphere of industry, from which they have partly developed. This is what Sir Paul Reilly, Director of the Council of Industrial Design, said in his talk to the second Ravensbourne Assembly:

I am sure this compartmentalisation of life is at the root of many of our troubles today, for it sets up barriers of incomprehension that need increasing effort and goodwill to overcome. It makes the left hand ignore the right; it encourages hoarding and duplication at every level of government; it makes industries sit upon know-how that should be shared; it makes manufacturers secretive and suspicious; it even builds barriers between a maker and his customer – for you could not work for long in my job without being astonished at the misunderstandings that arise in industry after industry between manufacturers and retailers, two sets of people who, one would have thought, should be on the closest terms of mutual trust (67).

The trend does not continue without opposition from schools, for one of the central aims of education is to nourish men and women to become balanced and tolerant in outlook, with wide interests: in short, people who are *complete*. If true breadth of vision could be achieved nationally, many of the extremes of compartmentalism would be avoided.

This is one of the strongest reasons for laying stress on a universal approach in primary education; that is, on what is often called 'integration'. By the blurring or obliterating of the academic boundaries between 'subjects' in schools, the oneness of all subjects is subtly communicated to children, so they never come to think in terms of sectors like 'English' or 'Mathematics'. Instead, they grow aware of *relationships*: how, for example, a coast-line and mountains can affect the history of a town; or how a white paper square can be made mathematically larger, by having thin strips added to it, at the same time as it grows visually smaller by being painted black. Children are encouraged to think comprehensively by coming up against the realities of relationships and exploring them. They may find that a poem can be related to a painting, or the strength of a linen thread to the design of a MOBILE. It is now accepted that unless a child learns through experiences that provide many opportunities for the positive development of his attitudes and concepts, he will not learn with real depth.[9] Primary education nowadays is about experience in general; children learn to range freely and discover things for themselves – which is the best kind of learning. They come to see life-in-the-round instead of little segments of life-in-the-flat.

With the mixing of activities, the old subjects – which are better called *interests* – take on a new multiple nature, becoming tools, links and starting points, while they also remain the centres of different kinds of learning (painting a picture is usually concerned basically with artistic matters, however closely related it may be to others). Such interests are *tools* with which other interests can be studied (for example, plaster is sometimes used for taking casts of animals' tracks); they *link* together by reason of the recognition of relationships and the unity of life; and they form *starting points* for activity in almost any direction (for example, the study of a bird's beak, which is specially adapted to catching insects, may lead – through a look at migration – to enquiry about Algeria, and end in a collage of the Rock of Gibraltar).

In this multiple role art has a great deal to offer, for it is never short of starting points or significant ways of exploring a school's environment. Drawing and painting provide obvious examples, and even stone carving can be used with the study of mathematics or geography.

If they are to gain satisfaction from learning, children need a motive that wells up warmly inside them as the result of personal interest and personal identification.[10] When my little girl of four was told to do something one day, she said, 'I can't because I don't want to' – which sums up the nature of one kind of inability. In learning, it is only when we really want to that we really can. Very often, practical activity sets powerful motives into action.

Whereas it is essential to recognise the advantages in stepping across boundaries, it would be a mistake to undervalue the peculiar significance belonging to each interest or subject. With regard to art, there are aesthetic and expressive components that must not be overlooked. Here are two examples of how art can be used in work on a theme without losing its special qualities:

A class of eight- and nine-year-olds is following a theme of 'conflict', and some children have chosen the fight on the bridge between Robin Hood and Little John. After research on their own in the library, these children have mimed the fight and written about it. Now they are making a painted frieze in which colour and a strong feeling of conflict predominate.

In a class of ten- and eleven-year-olds, a group is designing a town that is to be developed around the village where the school stands. After discussing the town's needs, studying books, writing letters and making surveys and a plan, the children have begun to build a model of the town in chicken wire and papier mâché, with special regard to functional and satisfying design.[11]

The method I have been describing – 'integrated teaching' – is not the only method with which children can be taught successfully. If we were to accept all that some educators say, most teaching methods that are not entirely up-to-date would be useless or worse. But teachers and children are more important than methods. No single system, nor single man, is the sole repository of the truth. Many inspiring teachers have used methods successfully that seem to us dubious and out-dated. A time will certainly come when progressive teachers smile at the word 'integration'. There is no master key; it is more important to have a good teacher for a class of children than a good teaching method (perhaps this is because a good teacher makes good any method he uses). Yet if we are to aim at the best learning situations for our children – and that has to be our main purpose – we must use the best means we know for reaching them.

THE PLACE OF THE TEACHER

Good teaching is not often direct telling. Indeed, one of the most successful ways a good teacher can use to draw out a child is to hold a personal discussion with him, in which the child is scarcely *told* anything. By his inspired questioning and by obliquely suggesting solutions to their problems, a teacher who understands what a group is trying to do can often stimulate the children in it to work excitedly and formatively. This oblique approach, where the children's interests are not laid down for them but grow out of their own activity, leads to discoveries made by the children themselves – which are always more valuable than discoveries made for the children by their teacher. The teacher needs to be like a minor god or goddess, of an immanent and benevolent nature, who is tolerant and just, always ready to evoke, encourage and make positive suggestions, and who provides a reassuring though stimulating environment.

A good teacher who is able to hold to the immediate aim of reaching the best possible learning situation in each lesson will gradually come closer to fulfilling what needs to be the overall aim – that each child should become as complete as possible.

SUMMARY

Primary education seeks to foster the growth of the free spirit and completeness, in opposition to conformity and compartmentalism. Within primary education, art activities can work as vitally as yeast in bread.

Drives and needs that are expressed and satisfied through art activities include exploring, making, dreaming and imagining. Art engages the whole person, in his feelings, his mind and in the use of his hands.

There are many ways of seeing, some of which extend from retinal (naturalistic) to highly conceptual, and abstract. A retinal artist interposes little of his personal essence between what his eyes see and what his hands do. A child's art belongs to a childish kind of conceptual activity, which must be respected by teachers.

The dangers of compartmentalism can be combated through teaching in a universalist, or integrated way, rather than by 'subjects'.

Art is not only an activity in its own right but also a useful tool.

NOTES

1. (58), chapter 3; and (49), chapter 3.
2. (47) gives an excellent account of the development of the concept of self.
3. (64), chapter 5.
4. (50), chapter 8.
5. (50), chapters 5 and 8.
6. (31), chapter 14.
7. See, for example, (8), pages 40–45.
8. (6) See particularly, pages 54–61 and 359–69.
9. (58), chapters 3 and 7; and (47), chapter 4.
10. (58), chapter 3.
11. For a broad introduction to creative work in primary schools, see (10), chapter 10 in particular.

FURTHER READING

Students would be wise to follow up the references given in the text.

2 Drawing, Painting and Printing

In the following chapters, I have dealt with different kinds of work that can be done with children of middle-school age, outlining where necessary some of the ideas that are connected with particular activities.

GENERAL PRINCIPLES

If we are fully to encourage imagination, visual awareness and creativity, we must try to avoid the lesson given in a vacuum. Moreover, in order to stress the singleness of learning and life it is essential that our lessons should be strongly bound up with the children's own experiences, questionings and experiments, both in and out of school. If we relate our lessons to what is interesting the children at the moment, they will not come to think of art as a separate and imposed activity introduced by their teacher once a week. Instead, they will begin to sense the single vast activity containing and inter-penetrating it. A theme rising naturally in the afternoon out of what a class has been doing in the morning usually has more meaning than a new one arbitrarily introduced without regard to class context. Rather than saying, with the frost crackling on the window panes, 'Today I want you to paint a picnic', try linking your art with something that has recently caught the children's interest (perhaps their imaginations have been stimulated by your description of a coal mine, or a port, or a battle). Or try introducing a snippet of topical news that you know is of current interest – an earthquake disaster started a whole series of activities in one school.

It is this *embedded* nature of many art lessons that allows them to be lessons in more than art alone. After all, different art techniques such as collage or wax resist painting – as poetry writing, or recorder playing, or acting – are often no more than different means of coming to terms with a single theme. The earthquake-disaster theme illustrates this well.

Of course, every line of thought creates dangers, and can sometimes cause artificiality through trying to form links where none exist. Yet it is surprising how readily art joins itself with other subjects. There is an especially happy affinity between art, poetry, story, drama and mime, which are all deeply involved with imagination and feeling.

Art almost always requires a visual stimulus (ideas-poetry links less successfully with art activities than visual-poetry) and for this reason it is wise to provide at least one visual aid at each art lesson. This may vary from a description of leopards stalking through a tropical jungle, to a piece of mime carried out by the children themselves. Mime is always a good starter because it helps children to live imaginatively in the skins of animals or other people. Even being a tree in a wind can give a child a new understanding that strengthens his expression in other ways. It is worth remembering, too, that opposites are linked. For instance, there are many points of contact between speed and rest, or summer and winter. Starters that contrast well with what has gone before sometimes provide the kind of new and exhilarating stimulus that is needed to keep the lessons sparkling. The general ethos of a classroom – its 'tone of voice' – is largely determined by the amount of interest and enthusiasm generated inside it.

Criticism

When a child is at work on something creative, should a teacher offer criticism?

So long as it is never purely destructive, and never a practical demonstration on the work itself, the answer is yes. A short positive comment at the right moment can often open up new possibilities which will help a child towards fuller expression and so aid his growth. But we should never help a child in a practical sense: we must not take up his brush to show him *how*. And we must also remember that in art there are very few rights and wrongs, especially for children. Criticism is better called *oblique suggestion*, and it should always come from goodwill. In most creative work, a teacher should try to stress the *experience* the child is involved with, rather than the way he is expressing it. For a practical application of these ideas, see page 112-114.

Assessment

Almost every teacher of juniors is faced with the problem of assessing the value of the art work done in class. This does not mean arranging finished work in some arbitrary order of merit, for in that way adult standards and subjective judgements become oppressive. It means, instead, coming to a conclusion about whether a child is really growing from what is being done or not. These few questions will help when trying to solve this problem. Although they cannot always be answered with confidence, they will create awareness of some important factors.

> Is this work within this child's ability?
> Does the child enjoy it?
> From your knowledge of what the child has done before, would you say it has widened the child's experience and understanding of any of these: expression, materials, shapes (flat), forms (in-the-round), design or colour? (With children of eight and nine this need not include forms and design.)
> What does your intuition say: Is the child growing by doing this, or standing still, or even shrinking back?

If, on balance, you think the work is successful, display it in the classroom. Since it is very difficult to say what a piece of work has done for a child unless you know him well, small classroom displays are more valuable than big exhibitions of 'Child Art', in which the products are always seen separate from their creators, and sometimes liked and disliked for the wrong reasons. A smudgy scribble may be of more value educationally than the most exciting or sophisticated piece of work in a national exhibition.

Starters

When giving thought to the introduction of starters or themes to a class, the central point to remember is that children respond best to something in which they are interested. It has already been suggested that linking art activities with what has gone before is a good way of maintaining interest and continuity. But sometimes it will be felt that a theme is either played out or irrelevant, and that something entirely new is needed. It is then that empathy must be exercised and the enthusiasm of the children caught by a theme close to their own experience, such as the story of an unusual old house near the school; or something close to their imaginations, such as 'the Space Race'. The teacher must then, if and when the theme appears to be sagging, question whether it can be further extended by the introduction of fresh material; say, a recent discovery or a fresh piece of news. Taking the first example, is it possible to move on to a wider history of other houses in the neighbourhood? Or, deal with what happened to the house, or houses, during the Civil War?

This is not to deny that a good teacher is able to generate interest in almost anything – a good teacher always has the power to bring subject matter within the children's grasp in such a way that it becomes their own.

Developmental age

It is useful to know what a child is capable of at certain periods of growth. The chronological age at which these occur is bound to vary from child to child, but a mean age can be established for each period of development, which gives a rough guide to what children may be expected to do. This DEVELOPMENTAL AGE holds very much more significance in most contexts than chronological age.

Children of eight and nine become readily involved in subjects where they feel themselves at the centre of things. With this developmental age group it is good to think of *I* or *We* – 'I went on a journey', 'Mum and I went to the factory', 'We looked for fossils'. Because they draw what they know rather than what they see, children of this age are still at the period in which they use special symbols for things (SCHEMATA): trees have a symbol of their own, and so have human noses.[1] Often their skies do not meet their horizons; their work is, in a childish way, conceptual. It is wrong to try to alter these symbols. When the children are ready they will become dissatisfied themselves, and begin to develop their work beyond the schemata without help. There is no conscious concern about design at this age, though pictures will often possess an intuitive sense of rhythm and pattern.

Nine to eleven is the gang age, when the work begins to show a greater awareness of the world as it appears on the retina of the eye, and the schemata become flexible and are personal responses to people and things. Differences of clothing become important in drawings and paintings. Awareness of pattern begins to show itself. Now is the time to encourage a sense of community activity through more group work – 'Designing a Town Together' or 'The School Visit to the Parrot House'. Art and Science can be integrated closely, and there is a dawn of interest in specific skills towards the end of the period.

From eleven onwards this interest becomes stronger, and craftsmanship can be encouraged more actively. Colour, form and design gain significance, and the children develop an increasing love for action and dramatisation. When a child shows interest in perspective or proportions he should be introduced to the principles governing them, largely through his own experiments. At this stage children need to experiment more widely and adventurously with colour and materials, and to look more closely at everything around them – from landscapes, buildings and figures to tiny objects under magnifying glasses.

Methods and materials

The use of a great variety of methods is not in itself a measure of successful teaching. A teacher who works arbitrarily through the activities listed in a book, for the sake of diversity, cannot be aware of children's needs. On the other hand, by having a wide knowledge of methods and materials, a good teacher is able to steer children towards those activities most suited to particular abilities and themes which will therefore be most likely to stimulate growth. For instance, in the exploration of a theme, one child may be at a stage to benefit from clay modelling when another child in the same class is finishing some pattern work that could lead readily into printing.

Because invigorating methods and materials should be mediums for feelings and thoughts, they should always be open to exploration, so they become *means for moving forward*, and not ends to aim at. And because something that a person finds out for himself holds more meaning for him than something he learns from being told, children should come to each new art activity as far as possible through their own discoveries. It is much better for a teacher to fire children with interest and then to suggest they should begin using the materials in front of them, for themselves, than it is to demonstrate. (But see page 80.) A good teacher is skilful at inducing situations where the class *comes with excitement* upon new methods and materials.

The teacher must be within reach, and must know where the work is going, so that time-wasting or harmful activities can be avoided. If the teacher goes away, or does no more than surround children with a warm envelope of encouragement, sooner or later worthwhile activity will stop. (Metaphorically speaking, the children 'work the ship' – they are in the crow's nest, the engine room and even on the bridge – but their teacher must be at the wheel.)

It is very important that children should have a sense of doing things successfully; therefore, if certain tools or materials are too difficult for a child he must be presented with simpler and more amenable ones.

Here are three related questions to help in assessing the value of a method or material:

1. Can this be used successfully by this particular child? (Remember that the child may be much more versatile than you think.)
2. Is it likely to extend understanding of the world?
3. Does it aid expression?

Of course, within any single method, however commonplace, there is plenty of room for personal discovery – which is clearly shown by what artists have done with brushes and paints. Indeed, the very ordinariness or limitations of an activity may sometimes induce exploration and unorthodox discoveries. It is sensible to introduce certain limits, at the right time, in order to narrow a problem down and to point a direction. For example, a lesson might be limited to the use of black, white and one other colour only; or to two or three shapes connected with previous work, to see what can be done with them alone; or occasionally to certain very simple materials, such as primitive people may have used, to see how problems are solved then. A teacher has to learn, both by reason and by intuition, when to ask such a question as, 'Have you ever thought what it was like drawing with charcoal you'd made for yourself out of willow twigs?'

In the following chapters I have briefly described some activities that have been successful in the past. The descriptions of the processes are for the teacher to try out and are not in a form to be imposed on the children. They are offered as *suggestions and starting points, for bringing children to situations capable of imaginative variation and development.* Because space is limited, I have confined these descriptions to essentials. More detailed descriptions of processes are given in other books, some of which are mentioned in the further reading lists and in the Bibliography.

SOME ACTIVITIES WITH TWO DIMENSIONS

In the list that follows I have selected a number of activities with paper, paints, cardboard, and other flat or flattish materials, which can be carried through by children between eight and twelve. Although the developmental ages have been given for which each activity seems best fitted, this does not mean it is suitable only for that age group; much depends on individual temperaments. Sometimes I have suggested starters, themes, or links connecting with other subjects.

Work in charcoal, pencil or ink

Charcoal is a free-and-easy medium that lends itself to broad and flexible drawing. It can be used successfully on newsprint or kitchen paper. Its unavoidable smudginess allows it to be altered by flicking with a duster, but makes it necessary to fix it afterwards with charcoal fixative. Brodie and Middleton supply a strong, thick scenic charcoal. (8 to 12)

Some children enjoy making detailed drawings in pencil, and this should never be discouraged. Soft pencils, such as Rowney's Black Beauties, are more sensitive than hard ones. Never use anything harder than a 2B (6B is very soft, 6H very hard) and ban

Plate 3. *P.E. Scene* 58″ × 73″. (Group work – 11 years.) Paint and some material. The figures are largely schematic but many faces show adult influence. The horse is particularly objective in treatment.

Plate 4. *Fishing Village* 50" × 90". (Group work – 6 and 7 years.) A mosaic of 'tesserae' cut from glossy magazines. Forms have been pulled out with paint. Adult help was given with the white.

rubbers. In general, pencil is a constricting medium, unsuited to expressive work. Do not encourage children to 'line in' their work in pencil first. It is better to work directly with inks, paints or materials.

Felt pens are delightful to draw with.

Coloured inks make a stimulating drawing and painting medium. For monochrome line-and-wash, try pure black ink and a pen, along with diluted black ink and a brush. Dilute the ink with water to five or six different strengths. (8 to 12)

Spraying inks around 'masks' (see page 39) made from card is an exciting way of learning about colour mixing and pattern-making. (10 to 12)

Good surfaces for ink work are provided by cartridge paper, non-absorbent writing paper and card. Using inks forms part of illustration (English, history, geography, science) imaginative writing, calligraphy, labelling and designing. Remember that ink washes, though pleasing, are expensive.

Using paints

Besides the well-tried powder colours, there are various kinds of ready-mixed water paints available today. Powder colours have the advantage of range: they can be mixed to any consistency, from very stiff to very thin. Their main disadvantage is that even when palettes are stacked criss-cross, paint is wasted and there is a mess. The powder *will* blow about. While the tube tempera colours have almost the same advantages as powder colours (they squeeze out stiffly enough for thick painting) they are less wasteful and messy, and very pleasant to use. Another helpful invention is the water paint that comes in plastic bottles; although this kind is only suitable for thin painting, because it cannot be thickened. (Try Reeves' Redimix.)

I have found the tube colours the most versatile. If the paint hardens in the tube, push a knitting needle through the stiff top layer and fill the hole with hot water. (Reeves' Tempera-paste)

Using paint can give great sensuous enjoyment. Experiments with thick and thin paint help in this, especially when related to a theme. If a group is painting a frieze, for instance, the children may try mixing sawdust or sand with the paint to make earth or

c

ploughed fields. Paint thickened with Polycell or cold-water paste can be expressive of thick, heavy things like rocks and tree-trunks, and it can also be 'drawn into' with brush handles.

Supports

Sugar paper is the most popular for painting in schools. An adventurous teacher will use many other kinds of materials, too, including different absorbent and non-absorbent papers, odd pieces of hardboard, card, cardboard, packing paper, walls and even window panes. And if there is a paper-mill nearby, there is likely to be plenty of cheap and unusual paper or card available.

Let the shape fit the subject: a rectangle is not the only shape for painting within; do not hesitate to cut the paper to the painting, or to paint inside a circle or hexagon, or even inside an irregular shape.

Brushes

The children should be able to find the right brush for the job they are doing, so keep brushes in jars according to size. In general it is best to use the biggest brush possible for the job in hand, and to use a wet brush on its own, or paint-with-a-brush for the plotting of a piece of work, rather than charcoal or pencil. Occasionally a child will think in areas of paint (or shapes) without using lines at all.

It is most important to teach children how to respect their brushes. Whenever they work with tempera colours (such as powder colours, tube colours or plastic-bottle colours) they should always wash out their brushes before putting them away. With the acrylic colours, such as Rowney's Crylas or Reeves' Temperapolymers, they should not only do this when they have finished but they should also have a jar of water beside them for washing their brushes from time to time while painting. If acrylic colour dries on a brush, it can be soaked in methylated spirits and worked out with the fingers. Always put brushes with their handles downwards in their storage jars.

Water

Too many lessons have been enlivened by the knocking over or dropping of jam-jars. The best solution to this problem is to use large plastic mugs (cheaper than enamel): they do not break, and their handles make them easy to carry. Cheaper still, though not so good, are the lower parts of plastic containers cut to size with scissors. Another simple point: when there is paint, clay or water to be mopped up, or for clearing up generally at the end of the day, a sponge is much more satisfactory than a cloth, which soon stains and begins to smell.

Each child should have a palette for mixing colours in. The best palettes have wells; but plates and scraps of plastic and cardboard can also be used.

Easels

Children are usually able to paint happily on the floor, on a wall or at low desks; but sloping double-sided easels are best for individual paintings on paper. Easels of this kind can be bought, made locally, or improvised from trestle-table legs and drawing boards.

Straight painting

Some visual starter, if only for the mind's inner eye, is essential for all works of art. Besides gathering collections of visually stimulating objects, it is a good idea to make a collection of visually evocative passages of poetry and prose.

Here is a description suitable for eight- and nine-year-olds:

We climbed out of the dark tunnel and found ourselves staring up at the towering tree. Its branches were loaded with apples, bananas and enormous pomegranates like crimson pumpkins. [If somebody points out that you normally find only one kind of fruit on a tree, explain that this particular tree is imaginary – or a freak, or in an unexplored country. Too factual an approach to the world at eight or nine is wretched.] The leaves were bluish-green and they carried long sharp spiky thorns. Here and there we caught a glimpse of a leopard stretched out on a branch, blinking down at us, and there were purplish monkeys. 'Heigh-ho!' a voice called from very high up. 'The captain!', whispered Betty. It was only then we noticed the door cut in the massive base of the tree, between its roots, and the little staircase leading up inside. 'Here's breakfast for you!', the voice shouted. The next second a pomegranate swished through the leaves and burst on Percy's head. He looked just as if he had washed his face in tomato juice. I glanced up – and there was the captain's bristly beard.

Stories and parts of stories, poems and parts of poems, can all make starters that link with larger themes and stimulate imagination. They must always be chosen for their visual impact and with thought for the age group concerned. Usually a story being *told* to children carries more vitality than one being read. Similarly, if a reader can look up at his listeners and, as it were, *tell* a poem even while reading it, the impact it makes will be stronger. Here is a fragment of a poem for use with eleven- and twelve-year-olds:

> The walls grew weak; and fast and hot
> Against them poured the ceaseless shot,
> With unabating fury sent
> From battery to battlement:
> And thunder-like the pealing din
> Rose from each heated culverin;
> And here and there some crackling dome
> Was fired before the exploding bomb;
> And as the fabric sank beneath
> The shattering shell's volcanic breath
> In red and wreathing columns flash'd
> The flame, as loud the ruin crash'd. . . .
>
> Extract from 'The Siege of Corinth', by Lord Byron

There are links in abundance here; besides art and poetry, these also stand out: history, geography, science, ethics and vocabulary.

Here is a short list of other visual poems with possibilities:

'Kubla Khan', by Coleridge in the *Oxford Book of English Verse*, No. 550.

The first verse of 'St Agnes' Eve', by Keats in *The Golden Treasury of Longer Poems* (Ed. E. Rhys), page 296 (Dent).

'The Tiger', by Blake in *The Oxford Book of English Verse*, No. 489.

'Apples', by Laurie Lee in *Poetry and Song II* (Ed. James Gibson), page 17 (Macmillan).

'The Paint Box', by E. V. Rieu in *A Puffin Quartet of Poets*, page 106 (Penguin).

'The Icefall', by Ian Serraillier in *A Puffin Quartet of Poets*, page 183 (Penguin).

Many starters for drawing and painting can always be found in the day-to-day work of a class: Are the children studying birds? Or ports? Or the Post-Office? There is sure to be something they are ready to explore and grow excited about.

Helping the inarticulate

In most schools you will find children who are relatively inarticulate with regard to artistic activities: they have few ideas and their ability to express themselves seems limited. This will be due to hereditary or environmental causes, or to both. Sometimes a child can develop 'blockages' from being told by members of his family, or even by teachers, that he cannot draw. Whatever the reasons for diffidence, a teacher can usually help expression by encouraging a child to approach simple materials, at first mainly in a spirit of experiment, and then in elementary ways that express something of interest. Although such 'looseners' will not cure deep psychological diffidence, they can help a child to gain confidence and self-respect. As the child grows, the discovery of more demanding techniques, and successes with them also, may possibly lead to such valuable self-expression that the established personal disturbance is quietened or even dispelled. In the following chapters, the letter 'L' after an activity means it is well suited to diffident artists. But beware of allowing a child to go on using a very simple technique for a long time: it could become a refuge instead of a way of encouraging growth.

Spatter painting (L)

Colours are mixed in palettes and then flicked from toothbrushes or bristle brushes to make patterns. After a child has made several of these, suggest that he uses shaped masks cut from card. The masks can be placed on a sheet of paper and the paint spattered around them. When they are lifted, interesting patterns and pictures are formed. (8 to 12)

Finger-and-hand painting (L)

Paint of a stiffish consistency is best. Let the children mix several colours together with brushes and then 'paint' with their fingers and hands, very much as their prehistoric ancestors did on cave walls. There is a directness of contact between the fingertips and palms and the paper and paint that is lost with a brush. Make sure that sleeves are rolled up and that overalls protect all clothing. Polycell or cold-water paste can be mixed with the paint to give it richness. (8 to 10)

Paint combing (L)

This develops from the above. Polycell is mixed with paint, which is laid thickly on to paper and combed with a serrated edge cut in a piece of card, or engraved with brush handles, rulers or similar objects. (8 to 12)

String painting (L)

Frequently a child is able to 'pull' a string painting that is more aesthetically satisfying to everybody than one pulled by an adult. The confidence gained from doing this can be very stimulating to a hesitant child. Take a piece of well-grained string of medium thickness, soak it in wettish paint and then loop it down in a pattern on one half of a piece of paper, with both ends hanging over the edge. Fold the other half of the paper over it and press it under a weight. Then pull the string out sideways. When the paper is opened out, delicate and surprising 'wings' or 'flowers' emerge. (8 to 12)

Fumages (blowing) (L)

This is another useful loosener. Very wet paint is blobbed from a brush on to a piece of paper and then blown across the surface to make a picture. Straws increase accuracy; but beware of children whose memories of sucking 'pop' through a straw become too strong. Good themes are 'Bonfire Night', 'The Great Fire of London', 'Forests' and 'Coral Reefs' – which also link with history, science and nature study. (8 to 12)

Friezes and murals

Group work directed towards a common goal not only instills

confidence but also gives the child a practical introduction to what working together and democracy mean. Friezes can be drawn in charcoal only, or painted, or printed with almost anything that has been dipped in paint; or they can be made as 'mosaics' from small pieces of torn or cut paper. Special frieze paper should be used for working on, or sheets of stiff paper stuck together on the back with sticky tape. Some enlightened headteachers may allow their children to paint on certain walls or windows in the school, and for this, acrylic paints are best.

Another type of frieze is made by sticking coloured tissue paper or cellophane over loopholes cut in black card, and then lighting it from behind.

Group work is best with nine-year-olds and above, but I have seen beautiful work done by groups of younger children. (Plate 4. *Fishing Village*)

Wax resist

Wax gives an elusive quality to a picture, and children are attracted by the apparently magical way it throws off a coloured liquid, revealing itself as a design underneath. The picture is first strongly 'painted' with a candle or wax crayons on rough paper, at which stage it may hardly show on the paper. Then a thin wash of paint, ink, stain or Brusho colour is boldly applied to the whole design. The wax, which will not accept moisture, stands out in contrast to the background of colour wash.

A variation is to rub the candle or wax crayon on thin paper laid over tree bark or heavily-grained wood before laying the colour washes. From this it will be seen that wax resist is particularly suitable for patterns and abstractions. Good starters are fossils, pieces of burnt wood, the foot of a hedgerow in spring, or rock formations – which have strong links with science or geography. (8 to 12: abstraction 11 to 12)

Masking

Paint spraying gains interest when used with masks. These are usually cut from stiff card and then lightly pinned to a support material, such as sugar paper. Thin paint or ink is blown in a succession of colours over the whole surface out of diffusers, hand-sprays or plastic hair-lacquer bottles. (8 to 12)

Diluted citric acid can be sprayed in a similar way on to a dried wash of strong permanganate of potash. (11 to 12)

Representation, abstraction and pattern-making

Most children enjoy making patterns. They give them a sense of order and stability; and they are linked to their schemata, which are in themselves a form of pattern.

Partly because of this, and partly because abstraction and pattern are very important in adult art today, a tendency is some-times found to discourage representational work even among children. Would it be wise for abstraction and pattern-making to push out representational work in the middle school?

As I have indicated in chapter I, children show a preference for naturalistic work (page 18) and they have a need to learn how they are situated within their environment, particularly with regard to people and things, by exploring it through their faculties. They *need* people, homes and recognisable objects in their lives; and these are so important to them that they seek to know more about them through re-creating and examining them with words and in art forms.

At first, from early in their art work, children do very much what the art schools do, but innocently, without reasoning. That is, they express what they know and feel, rather than what they see. Schemata are born that possess for them, I suspect, almost the truth of retinal representation.

But they seem to grow dissatisfied with their symbols after a while – 'It's not right' . . . 'He doesn't really look like that' – and they seem impelled to move towards an increasingly faithful expression of retinal experience. (An interesting parallel is suggested here with the development of Greek art.)

There is evidence that proper understanding of the sophisti-cated symbolism and relatively pure aesthetic content of abstracts only develops during adolescence (73) and it would be as wrong to deflect children from their natural preoccupation with retinal representation, by forcing the process of abstraction too soon, as it would be to force them out of their schematic period.

Moreover, too much pattern-making and abstraction constrict art work into something more, rather than less, specialised. The way forward for art in school lies in the opposite direction: towards closer integration with man and his many-sided life, and away from compartmentalism of the spirit.

However, there are some children of middle-school age whose powers of analytical thought are equal to the problem of consciously extracting significant elements from real objects in order to produce new and semi-abstract or abstract artefacts; and such children must be encouraged. As I have said, children enjoy pattern-making; and analytically–minded older juniors undoubtedly gain from a process in which their pattern-making becomes abstraction from such forms as evocative logs or fossils.

Anything that is related to their own experience and environment is likely to engage their sympathies; and even in analysis, feeling must not be forgotten. (Too often the new 'visual grammar' degenerates into an imposition of adult standards on children, divorced from feeling.)

All art must have within it elements of both abstraction and pattern. When a child, or a group, is ready to analyse (and where lessons have grown naturally towards analysis), an opportunity will come to ask whether anything lies concealed behind or within a retinal experience; and then some understanding of what abstraction really means may begin to grow in the child's mind.

Making patterns

The need to make patterns usually follows on naturally from the work being done. If a face-mask, a work folder, or a picture seems to ask for embellishment, then the best pattern and colour relation for the shape in question have to be found by the children themselves. Sometimes children will set out simply to 'do a pattern'. The everyday environment offers an inexhaustible supply of material for pattern-making – with its chimney pots, television aerials, roofs, tiles, machines, tarmac, trees, fields and rocks. And if the children use magnifying glasses they will find a multitude of unexpected patterns in such things as the inner parts of flowers, fruits and dry seed-cases. It is important to remember that patterns should not be copied from books or fabrics, and should not come too easily or be commercial-looking.

Good patterns fall into four categories, which sometimes overlap or mix.

1. *Repeating patterns.* Although these do not encourage much original thought, they often give confidence; and they seem to fill a need in some children for something elusive, which is related to stability and certainty. The initial nucleus of the pattern must have meaning. Letters, used with and without words, make good starters, and link themselves with English and calligraphy. Try using 'pens' made from rectangles of cardboard and dipped in paint or ink. (8 to 12: preferably 8 to 10)

2. *Varied patterns.* A few simple shapes are related together to make a significant design. Even a single shape can be turned about and altered in colour and tone through many variations. (8 to 12: preferably 8 to 11)

3. *Imaginative patterns* come naturally from the mind's eye and usually twist and turn and wander all over the picture space. Try working from a centre outwards, or from outside inwards, in spirals or in concentric circles. (8 to 12)

4. *Analytical patterns.* Once a child is able to extract meaning from objects through analysis, all kinds of interesting possibilities are opened up. 'Maps' can be plotted of the pattern in a rock face, or the planes in a lump of coal. Or a local landscape can be divided up tonally or chromatically on paper, in a study of balance. Or a solid piece of concrete can be reduced to flat shapes and colours on paper, linking with a study of area. It is a mistake to think in terms of one medium only for each piece of work: paints are often strengthened with wax crayons, pastels, tissue paper or card-prints (see page 45).

Mathematics can be introduced through progressions, and other exercises, in points or lines. A promising study, linked to science and geography, grows up around a comparison of organic with inorganic themes; for instance, tree-bark with a dry-stone wall; or animal cells, seen through a microscope, with rock crystals. (11 to 12 only)

Pastels and crayons

Traditionally, pastels are sensitive to very subtle nuances of colour and tone, and they have the advantage of being ready to use – there is no mixing in palettes or washing out with water. Their disadvantage is the tendency to smudge. To overcome this, they have to be fixed with pastel fixative; and each pastel painting in turn should be put under a clean sheet of paper before it is stored. (Rowney's Georgian and Reeves' Greyhound Pastels are to be recommended.)

Oil pastels, which do not smudge, and which need no fixing, are a little less sensitive and longer lasting than traditional pastels. They are closer to the wax crayons that have been successful with infants and juniors for many years. (Try Reeves' Pastenoil Pastels.)

Pastels and crayons can be used in a linear way on their points, like pencils, or else flat on their sides for broad work on coarse paper. They are most successful in layers, one on top of the other, when the colours mix deeply and shine through each other. (8 to 12)

Rubbings

By rubbing wax crayons over paper laid on one rough surface after another, children become sensitive to surface texture and pattern. Bark, bricks, wood, bicycle tyres and concrete offer interesting possibilities. The pictures or patterns can be built up layer by layer. Good subjects are Dragons, Monsters, People or Fish – which link with stories, poems and science. MOSAICS or COLLAGES can sometimes be made partly or wholly from pieces cut from rubbings.

Leaf rubbings are often pleasing as pattern; and they are closely linked to science. Take a well-veined leaf and put it upside down on a flat surface; then lay a piece of thin paper over it and rub the paper with wax crayons. After this, further leaves or grasses can be used to build up a significant design. (8 to 12: preferably 8 to 10)

PRINTING

The way a blot of paint or a piece of card or lino can suddenly double itself has a touch of sleight-of-hand about it for many children. *Squashouts* (L) are the simplest form of printing, which helps to make them especially successful as looseners with hesitant children. (There is always some art form that even the most diffident child can make his own.) A big blob of creamy and attractively mixed paint is dropped in the middle of a piece of paper, which is folded over, smoothed thoughtfully, and then opened out. Into the resulting beetle-like or flower-like shapes, further blobs are dropped; and the folding-over and opening-out process is repeated.

Do not think of these squashouts solely as looseners: they can also help with pattern-making and developing sensitivity towards colour and paint. There are lifted and ribbed effects in most squashouts that could not be gained in any other way. They can be used mathematically, too, to give understanding of balance, area and symmetry. Furthermore, like flames in the fire, they form useful starters for stories and poems, because things can be seen in them, such as faces or birds. Sometimes a coat of paper varnish, laid after a day or two, will make the mat tempera 'sing'. (8 to 12)

Potato cuts

Try these for pattern-making (see pages 40–42) or 'mosaics' (page 46). They are also good for fabric printing with water-based block-printing colours (which, it should be remembered, are not fast). Cut a potato, carrot or turnip in half and engrave and carve the flat surface with a penknife or lino-cutter. Dab this surface into paint, or brush paint over it, and press it down on to paper or fabric. Several different cuts can be used together, with a different design on each one. Reeves' Water-Based Block Printing Colours are suitable for all the print-making mentioned in this section. (8 to 12)

Clay prints

As with most art activities, it is best to introduce printing with clay as a challenge or a problem (see page 31). Present a group of children with a slab of clay, pen knives, lino-cutters, paints and paper, and ask the children whether they can discover a way of printing. The slab will allow them to make prints of various dimensions, which are easily altered, and to change a design quickly by putting in and taking out small pieces of clay. The clay surface is very pleasant to work on and the prints are both cheap and versatile. If a slab needs to be kept overnight, it should be slipped into a polythene bag. Plasticine can be used instead of clay for small prints. (8 to 12)

Card prints

Pieces of card or cardboard are cut into shapes and pressed on to paper to make prints. They can be used individually or stuck on to a larger piece of cardboard, forming a design. Probably the best way of laying colour on flat printing surfaces like these is to roll it on, but it can also be painted on with a brush. To print, either roll the card shapes on to the paper with a clean roller, or the paper on to the card shapes. Try using different papers, too. Simple patterns and representational, story-telling, shapes are good with eights to elevens.

Protect the card beforehand with a thin coat of Evo-Stik; it will not 'pull up', and it will be possible to gain depth through overprinting with thin, sticky colours laid in broken layers on top of one another. Different areas of card can be painted in different colours to make unique prints. If there is difficulty in taking prints, try burnishing the paper on the card with a wooden spoon. Prints are sometimes enhanced with pastels, coloured inks, or pieces of tissue paper pasted over certain areas.

Geometric shapes, and shapes selected from the neighbourhood, such as pieces of an old car or lichen-covered slates, make good starters for eleven- and twelve-year-olds. In order to avoid too cold an intellectualism, try to relate the study of the shapes with feeling – what is the *feeling* of a shape abstracted from an old carburettor? Is it hard all the way round, and cruel, or is it softened in places by merging with the colour behind it?

Leaf prints

Colour is laid on the undersides of well-veined leaves, which are then pressed on to paper to give a design. As with most forms of printing, over-printing – carried out as often as three or four times – brings richness and depth. Although in themselves the leaves are arbitrary, all kinds of imaginative and feathery birds and insects can be developed with them. Black card, or black paper, forms a striking ground for whites and yellows printed over darker and richer colours; and tissue paper laid over a print will modify its nature. The theme, 'Birds and Butterflies in a Tree', offers many links. (8 to 12)

Mono-printing

With this method, very watery paint is used for brushing a design on to a damp, smooth surface, such as glass or formica. Then a piece of paper is laid on to it and a print taken. (8 to 12)

'Mosaics'

These are sometimes approached through investigation of real mosaics and the tesserae from which they are made – which links with history and glass-making. After this, the children can be introduced to the possibilities of printed mosaics. Rich and intricate designs are made by dipping the ends of such things as bolts, rulers or straws in paint, and then pressing them on paper. Other useful oddments to print from are steel nuts, screws, nails, pieces of tyre or stone, carrots, turnips, potatoes, dowelling, cotton reels, string and the butt-ends of pencils and brushes.

Printing colours

Powder colour and tempera tube colours, mixed stiffly, are simple to use and easy to clean up; but the prints they give are usually less satisfying than those made with good water-based block-printing colours. Oil-based printing colours are unsuitable for middle-school work because they are difficult to clean up. Brusho colours give brilliant, dye-like results. Try mixing them with Polycell.

Tissue paper

Tissue paper, laid in one or more layers, makes decisive variations in all kinds of drawings, paintings and prints, showing clearly how colours modify each other. (10 to 12)

SOME THEMES, LINKS AND METHODS

Since collections of visual starters are essential, it is a good idea to encourage children to bring interesting objects to school – from pieces of old washing machines to Mexican sombreros – and to arrange their own displays (if possible, linking with themes in their other school work) on tables and walls.

Here are a few likely themes with extensive links: 'Gulliver'; 'The Armada'; 'London Bridge is Burning Down'; 'Don Quixote'; 'Beaks'; 'Snouts and Noses'; 'Prehistoric Beasts'; 'The Coelacanth'; 'Armour'; 'Machines'; 'Waves'; 'Hills'.

People are a universal theme. Try life-size portraits of 'A Miner' or 'A Business Woman', or characters who can be introduced with mime and written about in prose or poetry, such as 'Slinky' or 'Bossy'. Feelings, too, are themes. We can evoke them through music, music-and-movement, poetry or stories to form starters for patterns and rhythms of feeling, such as 'Struggling', 'Happiness', 'Peacefulness', 'Unhappiness', 'Violence', 'Gentleness', 'Hate' or 'Love'.

Museums

Visits to exhibitions and the local museum are often rewarding. Certain museums run a special Museum Service under which some of their less valuable exhibits are lent to schools.

Animals

Live animals are usually more exciting to children than animals in books. All the following can be kept in or near a school: gerbils (which have the advantages of being even-tempered, almost odourless, clean and frugal), terrapins, lizards, locusts, fish, goats, pigs, hens and ducks. Use them as starters for work in mediums that seem right for them. For example, a farmyard makes a fine theme for a 'mosaic'. Animals are clearly linked with science, geography, farming and writing. (8 to 12)

Colour

Children usually begin by wanting to use a large number of pure colours, but end by selecting and mixing. From early on it is wise to encourage them in the habit of selecting. This can be done by providing no more than black, white, crimson, vermilion, a medium yellow, a dark blue and a light blue. From these almost any colour can be made; and since mixed colours have more personality than un-mixed ones, all should be encouraged to experiment with mixing. If a child is reluctant to do this, let him try changing colours by putting layers of tissue paper or cellophane over one another in patterns.

Here are some of the many ways of extending awareness of colour:

1. Seeing the world through imaginary spectacles of a special colour, say, green or blue. The picture may be expressed in variations of black, white and the one chosen colour only. (8 to 12)

2. Making up simple colour patterns from imaginative thinking like this: 'What colour was the Thames below London Bridge when it was blazing?' or 'What colour was the apple that Eve found?' (Imaginative children of any age)

3. Making dark colours without using black. Dark blue paint or tissue paper is the dominant; usually these blue-based darks are more interesting than those based on black. (8 to 10)

4. Using a very dominant colour as the key to a picture. Van Gogh's yellow is a famous example. (This can also be done with a dominant shape related to the dominant colour; say, a horse, or an oval shape.) (8 to 12)

5. Looking at an object and plotting its colours on a graph. (11 to 12)

6. Balancing colours aesthetically to form a satisfying design, either in paint or with pieces of coloured paper arranged on a neutral background. (11 to 12)

7. Slides are useful starters for work in colour and pattern. Usually children will offer to bring some from home.

8. A candle will reveal new combinations of colours in a blacked-out classroom.

Magnification

The use of microscopes, or other simpler magnifiers, can expose unsuspected patterns and shapes that prove rewarding science-linked starters.

A visual music box

To encourage understanding of visual discord and harmony, take a big wooden box or crate and drill patterns of holes in the base and three of the sides, with a small drill. Remove the lid. Paint the interior white, and introduce a concealed bulb. Then lay the box on its undrilled side, with its open end facing into the classroom. Pass a series of threads through the holes, from side to side, in patterns of planes. These become clearer if old ping-pong balls are hung on the threads, and each thread is given balls of a different colour. These 'open planes' help children to form concepts of space and a wider understanding of pattern relationships.

Without the threads, the box can be used to make visual music of other kinds by the sensitive placing and hanging of stimulating objects in relation to each other, inside it.

SOME USEFUL AND INTERESTING MATERIALS

By testing a material, and by watching children using it, it is possible to decide whether it is worthwhile, and what it is best suited for. Here is a list of materials that I have found successful in one way or another:

Paints
1. The cheapest of all: dry pigments without binder, from Brodie and Middleton. Mix with Polycell or size.
2. Rowney's Fixed Powder Colour (in tins). Can be mixed with varnish or PVA medium, as well as water.
3. Reeves' Temperapaste. A tube colour.
4. Poster paints. Ready-mixed poster colours sold in pots. Dane's are to be recommended. As with most kinds of paint, you will need three or four times as much white and yellow as other colours.
5. Liquid tempera colour. Supplied in a large squeezable plastic bottle – Reeves' Redimix; Margros' Cromar Transparent Water Colours.
6. Water-based block-printing colours – Reeves' are excellent.
7. Acrylic colours. Mix to any consistency with water. Fast drying. They will 'take' on almost any surface and are tough

D

and flexible when dry – Reeves' Temperapolymer Colours; Rowney's PVA Colours.
8. Brusho Colours have great brilliance and staining power.

Pastels and crayons

1. Traditional – Rowney's Georgian School Pastels; Dryads' Iris Pastels.
2. Oil-based pastels. Relatively smudge-proof – Dryads' Filia Oil Pastels; Reeves' Pastenoil Pastels.
3. Wax crayons – Finart or Freart Cosmic Crayons. The large Freart size is the more valuable. Also, Rowney's New Art Wax Crayons.
4. Margros make powerful fluorescent oil pastels; useful for eye-catching poster work.

Inks

Kandahar waterproof drawing and spraying inks – Rowney.

Brushes

1. Bristle brushes are good for broad painting – Reeves' or Dryads'. Useful sizes: 4, 6, 8 and 10.
2. Squirrel and sable brushes are best for more exact work, though relatively expensive – Reeves' 'Rodea' brushes (Series 208) and Rowney's Series 34. Useful sizes: 1, 3 and 6.

Miscellaneous

1. Plasti-Tak (Unggi-Punggi) is invaluable for sticking sheets of paper and other light objects to walls, usually without leaving a mark – Philip and Tacey.
2. Cow Gum sticks paper to paper quickly, and is excellent for mounting.
3. For bonding cellophane, use Dryads' B275 PVA Adhesive.
4. Verithik Colour Sticks, from Margros, last a long time.
5. Plastic palette knives, also from Margros, are very much cheaper than steel palette knives, and adequately springy.

Last resorts

Newspaper or newsprint (which can usually be obtained free) used with charcoal, or with ceiling-wash mixed with Polycell and dry pigments. Or try painting a design in Polycell on to sugar paper or newsprint and then sprinkling it with salt from a salt cellar, or different coloured earth. After the Polycell has dried, shake off the surplus.

SOME USEFUL ADDRESSES

In order to gain an idea of each firm's range, it is wise to write for catalogues. In some cases, the following lists give no more than a hint of what a firm makes.

General art materials
E. J. Arnold & Son Ltd., Butterley Street, Leeds, 10.
Dryads Ltd., Northgates, Leicester.
Margros Ltd., Monument House, Monument Way West, Woking, Surrey.
Reeves & Sons Ltd., Enfield, Middlesex.
G. Rowney & Co Ltd., 10/11 Percy Street, London, W.1.
Winsor & Newton Ltd., Wealdstone, Harrow, Middlesex.

General audio–visual materials
The Educational Foundation for Visual Aids, The National Audio-Visual Aids Centre, Paxton Place, Gipsy Hill, London, S.E.27.

Film strips
Educational Productions Ltd., East Ardsley, Wakefield, Yorkshire.
Visual Publications Ltd., 197 Kensington High Street, London, W.8.

Miscellaneous

Brodie & Middleton Ltd., 79 Long Acre, London, W.C.2 – for large sticks of charcoal and dry colours.

The Cosmic Crayon Co. Ltd., Ampthill Road, Bedford – for wax crayons.

Dane & Co. Ltd., Sugar House Lane, Stratford, London, E.15. – for rich poster paints.

J. B. Duckett & Co., Sheffield, 8 – for Brusho colours.

P. K. Dutt & Co. Ltd., Clan Works, Howard Road, Bromley, Kent – for microscopes and magnifiers.

F. G. Kettle, 127 High Holborn, London, W.C.1 – for metallic papers and coloured tissues.

Philip & Tacey Ltd., 69–79 Fulham High Street, London, S.W.6 – for Plasti-Tak.

Strand Electric, 29 King Street, London, W.C.2 – for coloured acetate in sheets.

NOTE

1. (49), chapter 6.

FURTHER READING

Further details of most of the activities mentioned will be found among the following: Ash and Rapaport (3), Melzi (53), Lowenfeld and Brittain (49), Dimmack (23), Meyer (54), and Pluckrose (61).

3 Scrap Materials

Although, by definition, all art is artificial, some forms of art are less artificial than others. Because two-dimensional expression necessarily reduces solid reality to flatness, an element of artificiality enters into it that is not present in three-dimensional work. For this reason, many children find it easier to come to understand the world around them through working in clay or scrap materials than through drawing or painting. It is true that a clay model or a cardboard-box engine has to be considered from every side, whereas a painting is usually seen from one angle only, but this requirement is also the very one that allows greater natural scope.

In general, children should start with only a few tools, so that from early on they gain sympathy for their materials by touching and working them with their fingers. In this way they form a close understanding of the nature and possibilities of each material, as well as its relationship to the world they are discovering. It is only gradually that children find out how fingers become more versatile when extended into tools. Remember that it is best to allow children to follow their own paths to most of the processes mentioned in this chapter. Oblique questioning will keep them away from unproductive activities; and a confrontation with materials and tools can often be combined with a pointed problem. For instance, having confronted a group, which has experience of papier mâché, with everything needed for making a stick puppet, you might ask, 'Can you find a way of making big paper-mash heads on sticks just out of these things?' Again, most of the processes here are capable of a great deal of modification by children.

Since money is rarely plentiful in schools, anything with

formative possibilities that can be obtained free is welcome. It is surprising how much can be done with scrap materials: a variety of different collages, constructions and models can be made for little or nothing. Good teachers are good collectors who develop an eye for cardboard boxes, plastic containers and odd pieces of metal and wood; and their store cupboards become quarries from which their children select whatever they need. Through being encouraged to work out their own solutions, the children come to discover the peculiarities of each material and what it is best suited for. Does a cotton reel make a good wheel? . . . How strong is brown paper? . . . Will Polycell stick paper to glass? These are the sort of questions they should be asking and answering themselves.

Here are some of the things that are worth collecting:

Rags	Different kinds of string
Newspapers	Pieces of wood, hardboard and 'High-
Pieces of paper and card	light' insulation board
Cardboard	Nuts, bolts, nails and screws
All kinds of boxes	Pieces of machinery
Cartons	Stones and shells
Jam-jars	Reeds, rushes and grasses
Bottles	Wools and threads
Milk-bottle tops	Pieces of fabric
Match-sticks	Wire
Match-boxes	Old ping-bong and tennis balls
Magazines	Balloons
Wallpaper	Dustbins
Pieces of furniture	Pattern books

MODELS

During the middle-school period, much can be learnt through models; and it is probably in model-making activity that art links itself most closely with other subjects. For example, a study of America might lead to models of a Mississippi paddle-steamer, a Red Indian tepee, or a cross-section of the Rockies; and a study of the Industrial Revolution, to models of an early beam engine or a coal mine. Once you have made a model or a picture of something, you become – in a special sense – owner of it.

Cardboard boxes (strengthened with hardboard strips) make a good foundation for many models. The boxes can be held together with wire, brass 'split-pin' paper fasteners, Evo-Stik or Marvin Medium, and then embellished with parts of plastic containers, cigarette packets, corrugated cardboard or anything else that seems right. It is usually best to finish surfaces with one or two coats of water paint, or with different kinds of paper, stuck down with Polycell. If you use plastic containers or shiny cigarette packets, you will find that PVA adhesives, like Marvin Medium, and PVA colours, like Rowney's, are best for sticking and painting. A rub with Vim or a Brillo pad gives tooth to a shiny surface. Egg-boxes and polystyrene apple-separators evoke such surfaces as dinosaur skin, armour and rocks. Chicken wire and papier mâché are suitable for cross-sections (see page 64).

As with all art activities, the idea of exploration should be in the children's minds when they make a model. Whatever its theme, a model will tend to develop more and more personality of its own as it grows, resulting from the fitting together of volumes, tones, colours and textures. Children should be aware of the need to explore these qualities in order to understand them better.

Younger children like both fantastic models (such as dragons) and models from the real world (such as bridges and boats).

Although older children are unlikely to lose interest in such things, they should be encouraged to branch out into the purer forms of construction, where the stress falls on mathematical or aesthetic values. As exercises in the mathematical significance of area, volume or symmetry, pieces of hardboard can be slotted with a coarse saw and fitted together to express 'A Family of Squares', 'The Oblong Family' or 'A Skyscraper of Long Pieces'. The same slotting technique can be used for exploring the importance of a quality like balance, approached from the artist's point of view. Constructions made of cardboard boxes, strengthened with hardboard strips, are an elaboration of this idea. To be able to reduce an artefact almost to a mathematical minimum, while at the same time achieving the asymmetrical symmetry of the artist, is to master one form of abstraction. ('Asymmetrical' because an artist works by intuition rather than by mathematical calculation.)

When making their models, children will sometimes want to use pieces of wood, which means they will need saws and hammers, and one may question whether it is wise to put such potentially dangerous tools in the hands of some individuals. The answer must be to allow a child to use a tool he genuinely needs for his work, having decided, from knowledge of him, that he will be able to handle it sensibly. If he begins to misuse the tool, he is not ready for it. Tool-racks are invaluable, and so are boxes for nails, tesserae, buttons, rubber bands, cotton reels, and the other small aids to model-making. Try to establish a definite storage place for everything that is used regularly.

Here is a chart showing five ideas for models:

MODEL	LINK AND TOPIC	SOME BASIC MATERIALS	MOST SUITABLE AGE GROUP
Giant	story imagination	cardboard boxes	8 to 10
Early Steam Engine	Industrial Revolution	cardboard boxes toilet rolls cotton reels	8 to 12
Martian Creature	space travel planets	rolled paper or plastic containers old tennis balls	9 to 12
Working Windmill	wind	cardboard boxes dowelling hardboard	10 to 12
Family of Circles	aesthetic values mathematics	hardboard circles	10 to 12

Match-boxes and wire

Although matches are used less nowadays, match-boxes are still sufficiently common to provide an easily available general

Plate 5. *Crusader* 18" × 44". (Boy – 11 years.) Main materials: a plastic bottle, cloth and silver paper, mounted on Oxford paper. The knight and boats move towards the closed shapes of the castle.

Plate 6. *Bus Queue* 22″ × 126″. (Group work – 8 and 9 years.) Paint on paper. This picture is remarkable for the variation in scale of its figures, the wholeness of its design and its individual characterisation.

Left: – Plate 7. *Vicar* 14" × 20". (Girl – 10 years.) Paint. A sensitive union of a mild and benevolent person with a solemn fate. The picture came from a description of a vicar by the teacher.

Below: – Plate 8. *Elephants Chasing a Bus* 15" × 20". (Boy – 10 years.) Thick paint. A vigorous illustration to a story told by the teacher on the spur of the moment.

Plate 9. *Desert Cobra* 20″ × 36″. (Group work – 10 years.) A collage. Circles of embossed wallpaper and strips of material translated into snakeskin.

building material. They can be fitted together on their own to make small constructions and reliefs.

Galvanised wire is another versatile material: it binds strongly (especially when twisted with pliers), is invaluable for supports and armatures, and can be bent and twisted into spidery constructions for the containing and cross-rigging of space. A unique metallic surface can be obtained by cutting short lengths of wire and sticking them on to cardboard or wood. Wire comes in gauges (the lower the gauge number, the thicker the wire) of which 16 and 20 are the most useful. Florists' wire is also handy.

Straws

These make interesting, if short-lived, constructions. Let the children see whether they can join them with pipe cleaners. (10 to 12)

Expanded polystyrene

This is light and versatile but unless left-overs are obtained from tradesmen, not cheap. It can be cut with a sharp knife or a hot wire, modelled with a candle flame (test first, as some polystyrenes are highly inflammable) or etched by aerosol paints or Bostik.

Try placing stiff paper masks over certain areas of a polystyrene sheet mounted on a board, and spraying the uncovered surfaces very lightly with an aerosol paint. The parts sprayed are eaten away to depths that depend on the amount of spray used. Then any of the resulting surfaces can be modified with oil paints. For bonding polystyrene, use 'Marvin Medium'.

COLLAGES (L)

A collage (from the French word 'to stick') is a design made by sticking materials on to a surface, usually in unexpected relationships. Any material that is intriguing, or expressive of a chosen theme and subject-matter, is eligible for a collage – whether it be pieces of brick or pin-heads. Here are some of the things that can be used:

For the *support*: very stiff paper, cardboard, hardboard or insulation board. Or you can work straight on to the classroom wall.

For *rough surfaces*: pebbles, sand, earth or gravel.

For eyes, faces or circles: buttons.

Scraps of material, net, felt, feathers.

For anything *metallic*, such as armour, helmets, weapons or tools: metallic papers, kitchen foil, scraps of metal or milk-bottle tops.

Tissue paper, impressed and surfaced papers, newspaper, corrugated paper.

String, wool, thread.

Wood scraps, bark.

Pins, small nails, wire.

For a *roughish surface*, which *glitters* in certain lights: ballotini.

Leaves, rushes, grasses. (To preserve these, soak them briefly in Polycell before adding them to a design, and then varnish lightly with a clear varnish once the Polycell has dried.)

Scraps of plastic, plastic chips, vitreous tesserae.

For *sticking*, use clear Bostik, Copydex, Marvin Medium or a similar adhesive, such as Rowney's PVA Binder. Many materials can be stuck directly into one of the PVA paints, such as Marvin paint or Rowney's PVA Colours.

Collages are useful looseners for diffident children. As an introduction, let them draw in a sand-pit or sand-try, embellishing their results with pebbles and scraps. When they come to work on a more permanent design, most children will want to draw it in pencil or charcoal to begin with, as a guide. At first, it is not wise to discourage this, but as the children grow more accomplished they should learn to plot their ideas from the beginning with the materials themselves. Arranging pieces of cut or torn paper on a table is a good way of planning.

As with most art work, drawings and designs made in sketch-books are useful sources of ideas, arising naturally from the day-to-day work of a class. Here is an example of how a collage might be developed by a group of six ten-year-olds:

The class was exploring the topic of movement, and some lively drawings of animals had been made in sketch-books from a visit to the zoo and general observation. First, some ideas from the sketch-books were roughed out in a sand-tray, and united into a design of running and climbing animals. A discussion about the kind of animals to be allowed ended in a compromise: some were to be imaginary and others real. Next, a similar (but not a slavish) design was made from cut-out pieces of newspaper arranged on a table. Most of this guiding basis was transferred to a big piece of hardboard and stuck down with Polycell. Then the children began work on developing the animals, birds, trees, grass, ground and sky. Fabric, straws, parts of match-boxes and cigarette packets, match-sticks, net, tissue paper and feathers were all used. A galloping monster was built up from milk-bottle tops laid amongst metallic papers, and a dangerous-looking bear grew out of a moth-eaten fur coat. The trees were made from match-sticks, pieces of bicycle-tyre and fabrics. Tissue paper, in several layers to give depth, was used for the sky, with net added in places for clouds. (Net needs sharp scissors.) Tissue paper was also used for a pool; and the grasses growing on the rough sandy ground were made from string. When everything was stuck firmly in place, the collage was displayed in the corridor.

The best collages are usually metaphorical: that is, they make clear similarities between things that appear dissimilar.

Some techniques related to collage

As said, it is sometimes best to limit work to a few materials. Sacking or hessian forms a good support for string or felt applied alone or together. Try weaving different types of string into a piece of sacking. (8 to 12)

Delicate and sensitive designs have been built up layer-by-layer from net lightly sewn on to hessian. (10 to 12)

Colourful portraits can be made from pieces of well-ironed fabric stuck to stiff paper or sacking. With self-portraits, it sometimes helps children if they close their eyes and feel their faces before beginning work. If you hold a sheet of sugar paper behind a child's head and mark round it in pencil, it will show the class what 'life-size' means. (8 to 12)

Designs exploring area and balance, and closely related to the constructions mentioned on page 55, can be made by sticking pieces of hardboard or card to a firm support. The pieces need to be simple in shape, and to begin with some may be painted black and others white. In later work, the children might try to establish a clearly dominant colour, sensitively related to the dominant shape. (10 to 12)

MOSAICS

Mosaics are flat or flattish designs made from many small pieces of material.

The exploration of mosaics leads readily into mathematics, history and other subjects besides art. It forms a good starter for studies as varied as glass-making, Roman villas, the Byzantine Empire and geometry. Children who know what a real mosaic looks like will understand how it is built up from separate little tesserae.

In the previous chapter I have shown how mosaics form a starter for mosaic-like designs *printed* flatly in paint with various objects. Other designs, closer to the nature of true mosaic, can be developed by sticking materials to firm supports in the collage method.

Pulse mosaics (L)

Rice, lentils, peas, sunflower seeds, or differently-coloured sands, are stuck to card or hardboard with Marvin Medium. (8 to 12)

Cement mosaics

Something similar to a true mosaic is made when pebbles or pieces of coal or flint are pushed closely together into damp cement laid in a tray or box. The cement is most successful when mixed with sand in the ratio 1:3. (10 to 12)

Egg-shell mosaics (L)

These are made from scraps of egg-shell stuck in a wash of Polycell. The same can be done with paper punchings. (8 to 12)

Cut-card mosaics and mosaics made from 'old glossies'

A group of children engaged on a topic sometimes accumulates drawings from which a master drawing can be developed and then lightly sketched on to a big sheet of stiff paper. (Four sheets of sugar paper held together with Sellotape, laid on the back, make a suitable working support for a group of eight.) Let each child snip out a pile of 'tesserae' of a chosen colour from sheets of card or old glossy magazines. Enough Polycell should be laid on the support for about half-an-hour's work at a time, and the tesserae should be stuck into it to form the design. Discarded paintings and wallpaper sample books also make good tesserae.

Sometimes you will find that parts of the picture are not 'reading' because the tesserae are too similar in colour. To cure this, they can be 'pulled out' with black or white painted lines, although very good mosaics do not require artificial aids of this kind. (8 to 12)

MOBILES

These are decorative constructions that hang from high points in a room and move with the changing flow of air. They have been made from match-boxes, cartons and general scraps. One of the most enjoyable kinds of mobile follows a clear progression of size and colour with the use of an austere series of flat shapes suspended below each other in a 'cranked' or 'staggered' pattern.

For these mobiles, dowelling or 14-gauge galvanised wire is cut into lengths to make cross-pieces, and simple geometric shapes – sawn from hardboard and painted black or white – are suspended by strong thread from the end of each cross-piece (see *Mobile Arms*, Plate 18). As this requires some fine adjustments of balance, it is important to work from the top downwards. Fix a broomstick horizontally between the top of a step-ladder and some support on a wall, and then hang the first cross-piece from the broomstick with thread or thin dyed string. Suspend two shapes of unequal size and weight from each end of the cross-piece, and adjust the central suspension point until a perfect balance has been reached.

This will probably be enough for most children; but some will want to go further by suspending other cross-pieces below the first. The shapes look best when they diminish in size upwards or downwards; and the cross-pieces, which are held off-centre, usually hang horizontally. Some children will find other and unexpected arrangements.

Once the right position has been found for each suspension point, fix the thread or string in place with a blob of UHU glue or Evo-Stik. Minor adjustments in balance can be made by adding fragments of Plasti-Tak to the ends of the cross-pieces.

When the mobile is finished, transfer it to the high point in the room reserved for it – where it will swing in a leisurely, unceasing counterpoint.

As with other constructions, and also with reliefs, the guiding principle behind this activity can be mathematical, or aesthetic, or both.

Children should learn the important distinction between the arrangement of shapes by mathematical calculation, and the adjustment of shapes and colours to the requirements of feeling and intuition. Simple shapes like squares, oblongs and circles usually make the best mobiles. (11 to 12: for skilful children)

Simple mobiles

Simple mobiles can be made by hanging decorative shapes from wire coat-hangers, hoops, or wire circles (gauge 10 or 14) suspended from a beam. (8 to 10)

Woven mobiles

Stretch a warp of string vertically, at easy working level, between two horizontal pieces of $\frac{3}{8}''$ dowelling, with about half an inch between each piece of string. Then weave in and out of the string with thin bark, grasses, reeds, feathers and such seed-heads as teasels, to form a woof, which is intentionally left open and incomplete. Pieces of sacking and hessian are also valuable for this activity.

While the children are weaving, keep the dowelling secured to a wall or easel. When they have finished, suspend the mobile by a single piece of thin dyed string from a high point in such a way that light will shine through it, and it swings freely. The weight of the lower piece of dowelling, together with the weaving itself, will keep the warp tight. (9 to 12)

PAPIER MÂCHÉ

Because it is cheap and simple to use, one of the most suitable materials for model-making in schools is papier mâché. There are two basic techniques: *pulp* and *strips*.

Papier mâché is a building-up material, which needs a skeleton of some kind to give it strength and to hold it in place while it is drying. This skeleton, or support, can be made from cardboard boxes, plastic containers, sticks, galvanised wire or chicken wire. Probably chicken wire* is the most versatile, since it can be cut to size and easily bent to form the basic shape of a model. The closer the mesh, the greater the cost of the wire – but the easier it will be to lay papier mâché over it. Chicken wire with a half-inch mesh is usually the most satisfactory.

Polycell is excellent for making papier mâché. It can be kept for weeks, and a bucketful – mixed to the consistency of thick cream – goes a long way. While the Polycell is being prepared in class, one group of children can be shredding newspapers into confetti to form the pulp, while another group tears them into long strips between half-an-inch and one inch wide. When the Polycell is ready, pour it out into bowls. (It takes about a quarter of an hour, with stirring, to mature.)

To make the pulp, empty the newspaper confetti into a bowl of Polycell, stir thoroughly, and squeeze out the porridge-like mixture, first by hand and afterwards between old towels.

To prepare the strips, pull each one in turn through a bowl of Polycell, cleaning off the surplus by running the strip between two fingers as it comes out of the mixture; and then tear it into sections. The length of these will depend on what is being made.

The pulp can be modelled like clay, and small models are sometimes made with pulp alone. But it is mainly used for blocking in masses that would take a long time to build up in layers, or for filling hollows.

The strips are used for layering. Most models need at least four layers, and they should be put on equally to give maximum strength. Even those models made with pulp benefit from being

---

* When using chicken wire, be careful of the sharp points along the edges: for inexperienced children, turn these in yourself with pliers, or get responsible monitors to do it.

finished with one or two layers of strips. Sometimes it is wise to soak the pulp overnight.

Strips not more than three-inches long and one-inch wide usually weld themselves into dense and well-stuck papier mâché. If they are too long they often fail to stick properly, giving a crinkly surface. To ensure equal layering, use 'sporting pinks', or comics, alternately with newspapers. A group of children might be steered towards discovering this method for themselves.

Because papier mâché takes a long time to dry, it should be left on a radiator, or in a boiler house, for a day or two. Once dry, it can be painted with water paints, which often give the best finish. Sometimes a shiny, richer quality would improve the appearance of a papier mâché model, in which case it should be varnished with clear paper varnish, observing these simple rules.

1. Work in a warm, dry atmosphere.
2. Be sure there is no moisture on the model, the varnish brush or the container.
3. Warm both model and varnish first.

A group might be asked to find what happens – if anything – when these rules are not observed.

Papier mâché animals and models

A cardboard box makes a good beginning for an animal's body; its neck and legs can be formed from rolls of paper, and its head from a smaller box or a plastic container. After any hollows have been filled with pulp, the whole animal is bandaged with several layers of strips. There is unlimited room for ingenuity: I have seen teasels on their stalks used for eyes; and leaves, which had been soaked in Polycell, plastered over a whole creature and varnished until it looked like something from the bottom of the sea. (8 to 12)

Wasps and other insects, blown up to monstrous proportions, have been constructed from papier mâché laid on a wire framework and painted. (11 to 12)

Models of forts or castles are often strengthened with papier mâché, which is also well suited to the construction of cross-sections through mountains or coal mines. (10 to 12)

Plate 10. *Dinosaur* 20″ × 24″. (Girl – 12 years.) A decorative mosaic pattern printed in powder paint with potatoes and straws by a girl who found most school work very difficult.

Plate 11. *Girl With Monkey* 13″ × 23″. (Girl – 10 years.) Felt and other material sewn on to grey hessian backed by soft board. An energetic and commanding little figure.

Left: – Plate 12. *Dancers* 9½″. (Girl – 12 years.) Terracotta glazed with white tin glaze modified in places with manganese oxide.

Below: – Plate 13. *Two Pots and a Woman* 2½″; 6″; 2¾″. (Three girls – remedial – 13 years.) Terracotta glazed with white tin glaze modified with manganese or cobalt oxides.

People and big chessmen

These models can be made from papier mâché built on milk bottles or plastic containers. The heads are modelled in pulp and then secured to the bottles with strips. Ice-cream spoons make hands and feet. (8 to 12)

People of life-size proportions are sometimes erected on music stands. The heads are built up from strips laid on chicken wire, or on balloons which are let down and removed once the papier mâché has dried. Wool and string are used for hair; real clothes and fabric for clothing; and polystyrene apple separators, or painted cardboard, for armour. (10 to 12)

Masks and shields

First decide on the proportions of the face-masks you wish to make. The bigger they are, the more presence they will have. Model the main features in clay or chicken wire placed on a table-top or board, and then lay strips of papier mâché in six or seven thicknesses.

If you have used clay for your mould, remove it from the back of the mask as soon as the papier mâché has dried. The masks can be fantastic or based on real masks from Africa or South America. (8 to 12)

Shields are made in the same way as masks, and also link with history and geography. The papier mâché strips should be laid not only on the fronts of masks and shields, but also in several layers on the backs and along the edges. Sometimes it is best to discard modern materials and to use only those that are available to the particular culture in question. (8 to 12)

PUPPETS

The chief attractions of a puppet play lie in its imaginative and expressive possibilities. It also gives confidence to the children taking part, and links with many different activities – particularly writing, history, mimicry and mime. The puppets themselves are enjoyable to make, and develop understanding of characterisation, especially when they grow up with a play written by the children themselves.

E

The theatre

This sometimes presents a problem, although it is not difficult to knock one together from packing cases or lengths of wood about one inch by one inch in size (called 'one-by-one') and hard-board. (School caretakers are often helpful joiners.)

The theatre should be designed to stand on a table or on the floor, and it will need small curtains and simple lighting.

Here are some traditional ways of making puppets. Children will sometimes find other ways, or they will adapt one kind of puppet to another, and so produce something hybrid and original.

Instant puppets (L)

Basically all you need are a few clean white handkerchiefs, some elastic bands, and some paint. Arrange a handkerchief over your hand so that your index-finger forms the face and head of the puppet, and your thumb and middle-finger act as the two arms. Fix an elastic band around your thumb and the two fingers, and then paint a simple nose, mouth and two eyes. If the proportions seem pinched, or you are characterising a person with large features, plump the face out with material under the handkerchief. The children will soon see that further additions are possible, like small hats, hair and ribbons. Instant puppets can be used effectively with no theatre at all. (8 to 10)

Shadow puppets

Shadow puppets are cut from pieces of stiff card whose silhouettes are thrown on to a sheet pinned tautly across the front of a puppet theatre, a large picture frame or a doorway. Two or three powerful bulbs, positioned behind and a little above the sheet, are usually enough to give clear silhouettes.

Let the children design their own puppets. Although beginners may at first produce something too big or too small, they will soon gain a sense of scale. Stiff black card is the best material for the puppets, and important characters may be fitted with joints, which are moved from below by wires. But beware of giving a puppet any more than a single joint: there is limited room behind the scenes, and each wire requires a hand to move it. Secure the joints with brass paper fasteners.

The puppets are held up by rods of thin dowelling stuck to the card with Bostik or Sellotape. Sometimes, to avoid throwing a shadow from the rod, it is fastened to the card at right angles by means of a drawing pin pushed through the puppet from in front into the base of the rod. But in general it is wise to accept the shadows, thrown by rods and wires, as a natural part of the medium. If loopholes are cut in the card for eyes, clothing or other embellishments, colour can be introduced by sticking cellophane on to the back of the card, over the loop-holes. Good silhouettes are given only by puppets held close to the sheet.

Shadow scenery is also cut from card. The heads of bent pins are secured to the back of the card with Sellotape so that their points hang over the front to form small hooks which can be quickly hooked on and off the sheet. (10 to 12)

Stick puppets

The head of a stick puppet is made from papier mâché strips laid in five or six layers over an inflated balloon. When the papier mâché has dried, the balloon is deflated and withdrawn. A rod is stuck to the back of the head, and the puppet is given clothes. Stick puppets do not usually have arms, and they are too big to perform in a puppet theatre. (8 to 12)

Glove puppets

The first step in making a glove puppet is to roll a postcard into a cylinder slightly bigger than the forefinger of the child who is to work the puppet. The rolled postcard is secured with sticky tape, and then the main form of the head is modelled in pulp on the roll. Papier mâché strips are laid over the pulp to hold it together and to refine the features, and a little collar is built up in place of shoulders to give the clothes something to hang from. These should be big enough to reach down over a child's wrist, with arms of the right length for his thumb and middle-finger. Hands are made from ice-cream spoons or felt; if the arms are loose and the hands tend to flop, slip a small elastic band over each cuff. As with other models, string or wool makes hair, and the face and hands are painted in water paints, which can be varnished or left mat.

A more delicate head for a glove puppet can be built up by laying strips in several thicknesses over an old electric light bulb. When the papier mâché has dried, cut it down the middle with scissors, all the way round, and take out the bulb. The two halves are joined with three more layers of strips. (10 to 12)

ADULT EXPECTATIONS

The work that children do often makes adults uneasy: it seems so stumbling and unsatisfactory when compared with adult work that they feel obliged to intervene in order to raise the standard and to 'get better results'.

This attitude of mind has to be resisted. Few children are capable of working directly through a series of clear-cut stages in an adult fashion. The stumbling and awkwardness and beating about the bush are part of the way in which children learn, and are essential to their development. But at the same time they can often surprise adults with the originality and significance of their work.

SOME USEFUL MATERIALS

Adhesives and solvents

1. Dryads' B275 PVA Adhesive – for bonding many plastics.
2. Bateman's Household Adhesive – for felt, paper and textiles.
3. Bateman's Cement – for rubber to rubber.
4. Araldite or Bostik 7 – for a very strong bond.
5. Bostik 1 (clear) – for general light work. Fast drying.
6. Croid Polystik PVA Glue – general purpose.

7. Cascamite – for wood to wood.
8. Copydex or Cow Gum – for sticking paper and fabric. Fast drying.
9. Evo-Stik – for general purposes (including bonding metal). Leave for fifteen minutes before joining surfaces.
10. Marvin Medium – general purpose (including bonding expanded polystyrene). A PVA.
11. Polycell – for general work with paper, card and papier mâché. Thick polycell will stick a surprising variety of things.
12. UHU Glue – for general light work (including sticking plaster). Fast drying.

(Be careful with the inflammable adhesives.)

Solvents for Araldite:
1. If it is not cured (set), it can be cleaned off with a rag soaked in Acetone (poisonous).
2. If it is cured, it will soften under attack from a strong paint-stripper, such as Nitromors (poisonous).

Solvents for PVA adhesives, such as Marvin Medium:
1. If not hard, use methylated spirits.
2. If hard, use methanol (poisonous).

(For cleaning brushes with hardened PVA on them, use boiling water – it will do less harm than anything else.)

Miscellaneous
1. Ballotini – tiny glass balls that reflect light. For collages and similar work. Margros.
2. Banding Wheels (bench whirlers) – Podmore.
3. Jenolite – for removing rust.
4. Plastic Chips (in various colours) – for collages. Margros.
5. Polyfilla – for plugging holes and cracks.
6. 'Vitreous glass tesserae' – for embellishment and patterns. Margros.
7. Britect – protects metal from rust.

SOME USEFUL ADDRESSES
General sculpture materials
Alec Tiranti Ltd., 72 Charlotte Street, London, W.1.

Alabaster
Alabaster Products Ltd., Hixon, Near Stafford.

Felt off-cuts
H. J. A. Cropper Ltd., Warth Vale Mills, Waterfoot, Rossendale, Lancs.

Marvin Medium and tesserae
Margros Ltd., Monument House, Monument Way West, Woking, Surrey.

Malleable sheet aluminium, copper and brass ('metal foil')
J. E. Smith, St John's Square, Clerkenwell Road, London. E.C.1.

FURTHER READING

My explanations have been necessarily brief. For many other ideas connected with the activities mentioned in this chapter, see the following: d'Arbelloff (21), Dimmack (23), Hils (30), Johnson (39), Pluckrose (61).

4 Clay

When clay is in good condition it is so sensitive that it will respond to very light touches, which makes it not only suitable for exact and delicate work by skilled potters but also for the fingers of children. Every child should have some experience of it.

In using clay a child is able to give shape to a thought with no intermediary between his fingers and his material. This intimacy combines with the softness and natural 'in-the-roundness' of clay to give him a sense of immediate personal reality as he attempts to come to better terms with the real world through making images of it. For these reasons, clay is an exceptionally good starting material for young children, and also for diffident children of any age who find such sophistications as brushes and paint too much for them.

Clay is excellent for asking the questions 'How' and 'Why'. Children usually begin by merely playing with it, but soon this leads to simple experiments to see what can be made, and from these a teacher can encourage more ambitious experiments and wider questioning. Clay is so versatile that it is equally capable of fulfilling the needs of a class of infants, who may be pressing and rolling it, and a class of much older children, who are using it for models and pots.

Because it is always important for teachers to be sensitive to the lives of individuals, they have to see that subject-matter and material help the growth of children's personal interests and positive needs. The versatility and sympathy of clay make it well suited to the working out and exploring of crazes and themes. Girls tend to prefer people and animals, whereas boys like vehicles and boats.

As children who use clay grow older they become more

ambitious. From simple un-fired models they progress to decorated RELIEFS, coil pots, pebble dishes and ceramic sculpture, until they become fascinated by pottery's subtle processes of GLAZING and design. This is all right up to a point, but it must not be forgotten that pottery is no more than an instrument in the middle school, introduced to help children live more fully; it should not become a specialised subject in an insulated sense. By working with clay, children will come, with sound teaching, to appreciate the importance of good design throughout their surroundings.

THE NATURE OF CLAY

Strictly speaking, the word 'clay' refers only to the raw material dug from the ground, whereas the prepared substance used by potters is called 'body'. However, both categories will be included under the one word 'clay' in this chapter.

A lump of clay is composed of a large number of tiny coin-shaped particles, which slide cohesively over each other whenever the lump is pressed. This is probably the main reason for the plasticity of clay, which permits it to be pushed and pulled, and causes it to hold its form without crumbling. The sliding together and apart of the minute discs also helps to explain why clay is strengthened by compression and weakened by extension.

Before beginning any form of pot or model a child should be conversant with the three stages of clay.

The first stage is the soft and workable one, when the clay is like blancmange and the main form of the pot is built up.

The second stage is the LEATHER-HARD, or cheese-hard stage, when the pot can be persuaded to hold almost any form imposed on it by beaters or scrapers without sagging or cracking. So long as clay can be readily marked with a fingernail, it is still workable.

It is during *the third stage* that most accidents take place. Here, the pot has dried out until it has grown lighter in colour and very brittle. This is the brittle-hard stage, when nothing more can be done and pots must be left alone on their bats.

In order to avoid the cracking that sometimes plagues potters a material known as GROG, consisting of sand or tiny fragments of fired pottery, is sometimes used to open up the dense natural consistency of clay, allowing it to dry and fire without too much stress. (In firing, a piece of clay can shrink to between nine-tenths and four-fifths of its original size.) Unfortunately, schools often use clay without grog, so that models and pots which look sound one day, are found cracked the next.

Cracking also results from leaving models to dry on non-absorbent surfaces, and from damping models only on one side after they have started to dry. The principle to remember is that unevenness in drying causes stress, which in turn causes cracking. This means that you should always use absorbent BATS, and that if a dry model has to be softened it should be damped all over. To avoid the need for this, keep unfinished clay-work under polythene bags.

For general use in schools, Podmore's Buff Grogged School Clay (P1034) is excellent because it resists warping and cracking, takes a wide range of glazes and will fire successfully from a low temperature up to 1,300°C.

EQUIPMENT

It is best to work with clay in a Practical Activities room, or area, where a little lasting mess does not matter. However, with imagination, most classrooms can easily be adapted (see pages 101-102).

In this list of equipment for work with clay, I have used asterisks to denote the relative importance of each item; essentials being marked with treble asterisks.

Cupboards
*A damp cupboard. This is a cupboard with water placed in a trough at the bottom to keep the clay moist.

A drying cupboard (for drying out work before firing). It should be built around some source of heat, such as hot-water pipes. If you have no drying cupboard, use the top of the kiln.

Bins
***Dustbins (for storing clay). Place the clay in plastic bags and stand it on boards laid across bricks. Always keep three or four

inches of water in the bottom of each bin. If you have more than one kind of clay, put a dab of distinguishing paint on the side and lid of each bin. (It is not necessary to use more than three different clays.)

Enamelled bread bins. These are better than buckets for storing glazes.

Wheels

Banding wheels or 'bench whirlers'. These are more suitable for middle-school work than throwing wheels, and it is difficult to make successful coil pots without them. They are useful whenever anything is being made that calls for consideration from all sides.

Throwing wheels. Throwing wheels are too expensive for many primary schools. Kick wheels are cheaper than electric wheels, but they are also more difficult to use. If you do order a throwing wheel, be sure it has a seat. Podmore's Alsager electric wheel is to be recommended; and the same firm also makes a seated kick wheel suitable for children.

Cutters

****A single wire.** A length of wire, one or two feet long and with a toggle at either end, can be used for wedging and trimming clay.

A clay lump cutter. A wire stretched on a steel frame, which will cut through a big lump of clay like cheese.

Kilns

Electric kilns. It is advisable to fire children's work whenever possible. A shy child will often gain confidence from seeing his clay model transformed by the furnace into something hard and lasting. Podmore, Wenger and other firms offer a range of excellent small kilns. Podmore's kilns P5601, P5602 and P5603 will reach 1,200° C in the MHT* versions, and cost between £72 and £80. The P5611 (MHT) costs about £105. (1970 prices). It is wise to have your kiln and PYROMETER, if it has one, serviced every year through your Education Authority, which is more economical and convenient than waiting until there is a breakdown.

*MHT: Medium High Temperature.

Home-made kilns. A great deal of meaning is added to pottery in school when the children build their own kilns and fire their own pots inside them, instead of leaving everything to electricity. Moreover, the colour of 'biscuited' clay that has been fired in a good home-made kiln, where the flames have wound themselves around the pieces for hours, is much richer and more varied than the chalky uniform white or pink that comes with electric BISCUIT firings.

Ambitious kilns can be built using firebricks and metal bars. Designs vary widely; you can either follow the specifications given in such a book as Ruscoe (74), or help older children to design their own kilns. In either case, a study of the general principles governing kiln construction will save you time and disappointment.[1]

Trench kilns. One of the simplest ways of making a cheap kiln is to dig a trench, and then to arrange the pieces along the bottom under plant pots, which act as protective MUFFLES. A thick layer of sawdust is poured over the pots, which is then covered with sticks and logs; or coal and coke can be added to the fire, in which case the temperature may reach as high as 900° C within four hours. Try to prevent air from touching the pots by not refuelling until they are buried in ash. The way Nigerian women potters fire their immense ware forms an interesting link.

Open-brick kilns. These are built by laying house bricks openly, and without cement, in circular courses about two feet in diameter, one on top of the other, with a space of about one inch between each brick. Once the kiln is more than three feet high it is filled with about eight inches of sawdust, and the pieces are placed on this bed in layers, with sawdust all the way round each piece. At least ten inches of sawdust must be poured over the topmost piece, and the structure is crowned with an old dustbin lid. To start the firing, set newspaper alight on top of the sawdust and, once the kiln is smouldering well, put on the lid. It may be necessary to adjust the width of the chinks between the bricks with wads of clay, for in a strong wind the sawdust will burn too quickly unless the chinks are narrowed on the windward side. In still air the lid can be opened a little. The sawdust should be kept topped up for several hours.

Dustbin kilns. A similar type of kiln can be made from an old dustbin. Punch holes about half-an-inch in diameter through the bottom and sides of the dustbin, raise it on half-a-dozen bricks, and then bed the pieces among sawdust exactly as with an open-brick kiln.

Do not forget that sawdust firings are primitive and chancy – only about 75 per cent of the work is likely to be unharmed – but children will see what firing means in simple terms at a nominal cost. Pieces emerge from these firings black all over, or black mottled with grey, and can often be enriched by burnishing with a spoon and then by rubbing with candles, or pads of raw wool which still hold their natural lanolin.

Miscellaneous

****Plastic bags.* Farmers and market gardeners buy fertiliser in big plastic bags, which are useful for storing clay, and for protecting large pieces while they are damp. Smaller pieces are best kept in bags with draw-strings.

****Basins and jugs.*

****Buckets.*

****Aprons.* An essential for all who work with clay.

****Bats.* These are used to support models and pots. Since they must not warp, make them out of marine plywood, obeche or (least satisfactorily) hardboard. The best potteries have bats that slip in and out of the damp cupboard to form sliding shelves.

***Storage space (with shelves). It is wise to keep a section of your store-room partitioned off as a pottery store. At least one shelf should be reserved for the exclusive use of each group of children.

***Staffordshire cones.* These measure temperature by 'squatting' (bending over). A cone is more reliable than a kiln pyrometer. Cone 010 squats at 900° C, Cone 1 at 1,100° C and Cone 4 at 1,160° C, and there are many others.

***Kiln shelves.* All but the smallest kilns need shelves, and these are usually supplied by the makers.

***A wedging slab.* Clay is prepared by pummelling and kneading on a firm absorbent surface. The better wedging slabs are made from paving stones supported by bricks, or from slates taken from old billiard tables. If you have no slab, use the floor. Lumps of clay can be cut on a piano wire stretched diagonally from the wall down to the front of the slab.

**Sponges.* Small potters' sponges are used with a throwing wheel; larger sponges are better than cloths for clearing up.

**Sieves* (120-mesh, *80-mesh and **40-mesh). These are used with slips and glazes, which are brushed through them with

**Sieve brushes.*

Slip trailers. See pages 87-88.

Kidneys. Kidney-shaped pieces of metal or rubber, which scrape and smooth.

A galvanised-iron bath (for used clay).

Decorating brushes. These are used for painting pieces in a leather-hard or biscuit state.

Modelling tools.

Muffles and saggars. Pre-fired clay boxes in which pieces are shut up to protect them from direct heat and flames.

Sludge trays. These are made from plaster, and speed up the process of drying out wet clay.

A pugmill. An electric or hand-driven machine that is expensive to buy but economical to use in the long run, because it enables old clay to be reconstituted by pugging into a dense and uniform mass.

OTHER MODELLING MATERIALS

Although clay is the best material for most plastic modelling in schools, there are certain alternatives with specific advantages. Salt-and-dough, which is often given to young children, is clean and extremely cheap. Plasticine and Clayola offer varied colours that run right through the material itself. They require very little preparation, and are good for making small, accurate and colourful models. Moreover, they do not break easily, they are relatively clean and can be used again.

PREPARING CLAY

Before a lump of clay is used it must be rendered as workable as possible. If it is part of a consignment supplied by a firm, it is not likely to need much preparation; but any clay in poor condition should first be pugged.

Pugging

This process brings clay that is old and dry back to its original crude state of workability. The clay is either put through a pugmill, or chopped repeatedly with a spade and watered.

Kneading and wedging

When the clay has become uniformly soft it is slammed down on to a wedging slab, kneaded, and cut with a wire until large air bubbles and 'foreign bodies' have been removed, and the whole mass is generally amenable to modelling. After each cut, the back of one half of the mass is slammed on to the face of the other half. Children should choose lumps for wedging that are not too heavy for them. At first they will greatly enjoy slapping and slamming the clay, but if allowed to go on for too long, it becomes pointless and quickly palls.

STOCKS

These three varieties should meet the usual requirements of a middle school:

1. Podmore's Buff Grogged School Clay (P1034)
2. Podmore's Red Terra Cotta Clay (P1033)
3. Potclays' Ivanhoe Tile Clay

THREE APPROACHES

There are three ways of approaching clay-work in school.

The cycle

A teacher who adopts this approach will show the children what firing a pot means, from start to finish, through practical means.

After a strong seam of local clay has been found, the top-soil is cleaned off, the clay is dug out, and left to dry. When it has become brittle-dry, it is hammered into crumbs and put into a bucket or dustbin, covered with water, and left for several days. It is then pugged to a watery sludge. This is passed through a riddle and a 40-mesh sieve, and poured into a sludge tray, or on to a large cement or plaster bat, which absorbs the moisture from the clay. After a day or two it can be kneaded and wedged with an addition of about ten per cent sand as grog.

If the clay has not been used before, it must next be modelled into little bars, and tested in the kiln to see how it reacts to various temperatures; for sometimes a local clay will blister or bloat without the addition of grog in a proportion of twenty per cent, or even more. The best temperature at which to fire a clay is 40°–50° C below the level at which it begins to distort.

Once the clay has been tested satisfactorily it has reached the stage where a teacher using the 'aesthetic' approach begins (see next paragraph). It is modelled and decorated, fired to its first (biscuit) temperature, glazed, and then given its final GLOST firing, in which – as far as possible – the glaze is made from local materials.

The whole process takes time and can be laborious.

The aesthetic approach

Here a teacher buys clay and glazes ready-mixed from the suppliers, which allows scope for work on a large variety of pieces. It will also be possible to lay more stress on the value of expressive form and decoration than when everyone is deeply involved in basic practical matters.

(When buying ready-mixed glazes, a teacher should make sure they are suitable for the type of clay to be used. Crazing of the glazed surface and other troubles can be avoided by following the manufacturers' recommendations.)

The compromise

Probably the most realistic approach is to do a limited number of experiments with local materials, to consider all clay-work aesthetically and to link it always with wider activities. In this way the children are made aware of some of the processes involved in pottery without spending too long on each, and these rewarding experiences will lead to others if the children write to suppliers and museums, estimate and record costs, and study some of the pottery of Crete, Greece, Persia, China and Britain.

Many opportunities arise in clay-work for children to explore and discover methods and materials for themselves. There is a distinction between discovery within an accepted method (for instance, slip trailing) and discovery of the method itself. Whenever possible, it is best to present children with tools, materials and a particular problem, and then to allow them to tackle it in their own way. Sometimes this is unwise – for example, when the time comes for firing a kiln; and the coiling, slipping and glazing processes are best demonstrated at least once. On the other hand, children can discover a great deal about clay, slips and even glazes, for themselves, so long as their teacher directs their progress. Good teachers know when to demonstrate, when to intervene and when to leave children alone. Once again, it must be stressed that the methods described here are offered as starting points for discovery, which are capable of personal modification.

SOME THINGS THAT CAN BE MADE IN CLAY
General modelling

Although it is surprising how involved a child can become in modelling a pot 'for putting mum's flowers in', it is usually true that models of people, animals and other objects hold more significance for younger children than pots. There is always a danger that commercial models will form a source of cheap second-hand ideas for those children who are good mimics; and this can best be countered – as with almost all art activities – by following other themes that are significant and topical for the children themselves.

Ideally almost everything should be fired, but with a limited stock of clay a teacher will be obliged to explain to the class that if everyone's model is put in the kiln then no clay will be left. Consequently, some of the older models must be broken up. But never destroy any piece of work in front of children.

Good modelling sticks can be made from pieces of split and sandpapered bamboo; and bits of glass can be used for eyes, and

Left: – Plate 14. *Crouching Boy 6"*. (Boy – 10 years.) Expanded polystyrene carved with a knife and sandpaper files, and painted with poster colour.

Below: – Plate 15. *Stone Horse 9" high × 9½" long*. (Boy – 10 years.) The limestone was carved with stone chisels and finished with small files (rifflers).

Plate 16. *Knights* 12″ *high*. (Boys – 10 and 11 years.) Main materials: silver paper and cloth around a core of crumpled newspaper.

other decorative features, so long as they are fired over 1,040 °C.

To avoid cracking in the kiln, try to ensure that no article is more than one-and-a-half inches thick.

Work with clay almost always involves making something without an environment, which means that children who think of the world as a series of separate significant objects begin with a small advantage over those who see it more in the way a painter does – as a unified whole. Moreover, those who tend to *pull out* from a lump of clay to form a model have an advantage over those who *stick on* pieces: it is more difficult to avoid cracking and breaking off with this 'synthetic' technique.

This does not mean, however, that children have to be persuaded to pull out in preference to sticking on, which carries advantages of its own once it has been mastered. Instead, each child must be allowed to find his own personal way of achieving his aim. Most children tend to combine the two methods, with a bias towards one or the other.

Models are more likely to survive the fire if their joins are painted with SLURRY ('clay glue'), which is a mixture of clay and water in roughly equal parts.

People and animals relate to many themes and activities, and children should be encouraged to model them in action as well as in repose. (8 to 12)

At first it is not easy for children to conceive of a disembodied head, but after a while they will usually come to understand how shoulders form a support to what is the most expressive part of a person, his face, and how this support can be flattened to form a base. Self-portraits of children when they are happy, sad, tired or angry bring pleasure and understanding. At first, portrait heads need not be more than a few inches high; later they can be coiled (see page 84) to any reasonable size. (9 to 12)

For figure work, brief poses that are held for only a minute or two, and moving poses, and poses that are described without being seen, are more suitable than the longer, stiffer poses used in traditional drawing. (11 to 12)

F

Thumb pots (L)

Making thumb pots forms a sound introduction to all clay-work, being most successful when it arises naturally and significantly from other activities.

Make a hole with your thumb in a ball of clay, and then refine the walls by widening the hole until you have modelled a small pot. If you spend more than about fifteen minutes on each pot there is a risk that its freshness of form will be lost. Any small hair-cracks that develop in the clay should be damped and smoothed out with a little water. Seed-heads and pebbles make good starters, and the pottery of the Beaker Folk is an interesting link with history. (8 to 10)

Tiles

These offer scope for many different designs, which can either be confined to single tiles or built up in groups.

First you will need a 'skin', which is a flat layer of clay that has been rolled out with a rolling pin. Cut the skin with a ruler or template and the blunt side of an old knife, or with a tile-cutter, then trim the edges, and the tile is ready for decoration. This can be carried out in many different ways (see pages 86–89 for some ideas). Impressing a tile with significant objects such as fingertips, spoon handles, or the heads of bolts, gives pleasing results; or try dipping a leather-hard tile in slip (see page 87), and then brushing or trailing a thick contrasting slip over the resulting layer. Tiles can be made as squares, triangles, or other geometrical shapes; or flat patterns, taken from such shapes as chimneys, petals or fossils can be incised or impressed into skins, which are cut into sympathetic shapes, biscuited, and then developed with glass or glazes.

When experiments are being made with glazes it is easier to use a small tile for testing than a pot, although I have sometimes found that what seems a promising glaze on a horizontal tile turns out disappointingly on the vertical side of a pot.

Because tiles are flat and relatively thin, they lack resistance to the stresses imposed on clay when it shrinks during drying or in the kiln, and this often leads to warping. But Ivanhoe Tile Clay, which is heavily grogged, cuts warping to a minimum, especially if weights are placed at the sides and corners of the tiles while they are drying and they are turned upside down the moment they begin to curl. They are also less likely to warp in the biscuit firing if packed on top of one another. (8 to 12)

Clay reliefs

Clay reliefs are closely linked with tiles and collages. Be careful to make them the right thickness for their flat area, because a relief that is too thin will warp, and one that is too thick will crack. As said, a thickness of between half-an-inch and an inch-and-a-half is normally safe. Reliefs can be incised with a point, impressed with interesting objects, scratched, painted or dabbed with slips, or built up or cut away. It is also possible to fire them with marbles or pieces of glass laid in surface depressions, or to stick on such embellishments as vitreous tesserae, after firing. If firing glass in the kiln be careful that it does not run down on to a shelf or an element, where it will do great harm.

Here are some suggestions for starters for work with reliefs:

'The Surface of the Moon'
'The Floor of the Sea'   } 8 to 12
'Tree Bark'

'Birds and Flight Shapes'
'One Shape Growing Out of Another'
'Cogwheels' (from a clock or bicycle)   } 9 to 12
'Natural against Man-Made'

'Organic against Inorganic'
'Straight Lines that Change to Curves, across the
    Relief'
'Lines of Force in an Opening Plant'   } 10 to 12
    (i.e. the children plot the direction in which the
    forms are growing, and so make a pattern)
'Squares that Grow into Circles'

Ceramic jewellery (L)

The small scale of jewellery often comes as a pleasant change to children who have been 'working big', and it is not only girls who enjoy making pendants, earrings and brooches out of clay.

Simple shapes are cut from a thin skin of clay, decorated, fired to biscuit, glazed and then fired again. Araldite or Bostik 7 will stick clips and pins to the backs of the pieces. (8 to 12)

Coil pots

When a child has learned to use his hands a little, and has begun to think sensitively about design, he is likely to gain insight and pleasure from making coil pots. Some earlier experience with models or thumb pots will help, and he will be well advised to make drawings of the shape he is aiming at before he begins to wedge his clay. He should aim at the big simplicities and a natural growth of form through the pot. All kinds of starters are used for coil pots. Stones, pebbles, sunflower heads, and the seed-heads of poppies, have all been successful.

In general, coil pots are simpler to make than wheel-thrown pots, and are likely to be more successful in schools. After wedging, the clay is rolled out into long sausages – thick for big pots and thinner for smaller ones. Then a circular base is made from a ball of clay pressed out on to a piece of sugar paper laid on a banding wheel. (If none is available, a bat will do instead.) After this, the coiling begins. Since the coils are modified and refined later, they need not be uniform. In coiling, the wheel or bat is twisted in an anti-clockwise direction, and the coil is laid first on the base in a circle, and then on to itself, in *courses*, with the left hand doing most of the work and the right holding up the tail of the coil. When a circular wall has grown up a little way the coils are scraped, or *luted* together with fingers or scrapers; after which further coils are added. If the pot becomes too wide at this stage, its diameter will have to be narrowed by *pleating*. When it looks as if it will sag or bend if any more coils are laid, it is left to dry. Intelligent use of a plastic bag prevents the lower parts from drying too hard before the top parts are finished.

When the wall has become leathery through drying, it must be roughened along the top edge, and damped with slurry, before it can be built up further by coiling into the shoulders, neck and lip. As soon as the whole pot is leather-hard it is modified with wooden beaters (for the outside), wooden spoons (for the inside), GRIFFONS, scrapers, old hacksaw blades, or steel or rubber kidneys, until its form is expressive and significant throughout. Sometimes the coils can be left as decorative elements.

If cracking develops in a pot, it is almost certainly due to uneven drying. Cracks can be repaired with slurry so long as the clay is leather-hard. Since wet clay on dry clay inevitably leads to trouble, the only way of treating cracked brittle-hard clay is to rub dry powdered clay into the cracks. This is only wise when the pot is to be fired to STONEWARE in its last firing. With EARTHEN-WARE, use Wenger's Biscuit Stopping after the piece has been biscuited. It goes into cracks like putty and can be glazed when dry. (For biscuit, see page 90.)

The personality of a pot must always be kept in mind. Here are some considerations to discuss: when a pot has both a foot and a lip, a light foot asks for a light lip; since decoration draws attention, confine it to the most important parts; the shapes between and around the decorative motifs are as significant as the motifs themselves; handles need to grow from the main form.

And here are three questions to ask about a finished pot:

Is this pot suited to the clay from which it is made?
Is it suited to the purpose for which it has been made?
Is it a pot with an expressive personality?

(10 to 12)

Pebble dishes and slab pots

Skins of between a twelfth– and a quarter-of-an-inch in thickness are suitable for pebble dishes and slab pots. The best way of making a skin is to use graded sticks with a cheese wire; but for schools a more realistic way is to roll a clay ball flat with a rolling pin, which is kept level by two wooden or hardboard 'rails' of the right thickness placed opposite each other on either side of the clay. To stop the skin from sticking, keep pieces of sugar paper between the clay and the table, and the clay and the rolling pin.

A pebble dish is made by pressing a skin on to a large smooth pebble. If the edges are not trimmed a little above the pebble's equator the skin will have to be slit in order to pull it away. The dish should be taken off the pebble as soon as it is able to hold its form, otherwise it is likely to crack. Pebble dishes give many opportunities for decoration with slips and glazes. (8 to 12)

A slab pot requires careful design, and the preparation of card templates for the base and sides, which are cut by following around the templates on a skin with the blunt side of a knife. The pieces are put together with slurry once they are leather-hard. (10 to 12)

To make a rattle, drop a clay ball inside a pebble dish and then stick another dish, from the same pebble, on top of the first, with slurry. Skins are also sometimes bent and joined to make bells. (9 to 12)

Ceramic sculpture

Older children can be introduced to certain themes and starters that encourage them into thinking beyond pot forms, while still using a coiling or slab technique. In this, a VISUAL MUSIC BOX (page 49), displaying stimulating objects brought in by the children, often starts new trains of thought through its presentations of varying patterns of shapes. An interesting introduction to ceramic sculpture is the cutting of a series of holes, which grow progressively bigger, in a coiled cylinder. The holes can be of any reasonable size or number. Gourds, rock strata and bird shapes are good starters; and geometrical units, stuck together before or after firing, link closely with the constructions described on page 55. (11 to 12)

DECORATION

When children come to decorate their pieces, they find many opportunities for personal discovery and expression. At first, it is wise to let them have their heads; but after a while they will begin to look for principles by which their work may be judged. With regard to a pot, the area that usually asks for embellishment is the one that is most seen; if you decorate a pot all over, its form will be challenged, and this may seriously detract from the whole, because form is the essential supporting structure that decoration should complete and enhance, rather than cancel out through competition. A taut form may ask for precise decoration, and a generous form for something more spontaneous. Certain pots need glazing to bring out their full personality; others are better left mat. Here are some ways of decorating leather-hard clay.

Slips

When clay and water are mixed to a cream-like consistency, they are known as slip. This is left in its natural colour, or stained with a metal-oxide Slip Stain or Body Stain. Slips are used relatively thinly for brushing on to pots or for dipping; and thickly with slip trailers, or for inlaying.

Interesting surfaces, which are best kept unglazed (and which therefore need only one firing) are developed by openly dabbing one slip on top of another with a small sponge. If one of the slips is coppery, and the body of the pot is allowed to show through, the variations are likely to be particularly satisfying.

Here are the constituents of four different slips:

1. *A coppery slip*: 1 lb of ball clay and 5 ozs of copper carbonate.
2. *A dark slip*: $\frac{1}{4}$ lb powdered red clay, $\frac{1}{4}$ lb ball clay, $\frac{1}{2}$ oz red iron oxide and 2 ozs manganese oxide.
3. *A white slip*: 1 lb ball clay and 1 lb china clay.
4. *A blue slip*: 14 ozs ball clay, 2 ozs powdered red clay and 2 ozs Podmore's P4508 Cornflower Blue stain.

Weigh the materials dry, mix them with water and sieve the mixture, first through a 40-mesh and then through an 80-mesh sieve.

White tin glazes pick up the colour of underlying slips and pigments in pleasing ways.

Because slip is succulent in character, it looks best when thick enough to be opaque, and this remains true even when it is dabbed openly, for each spot of slip should not in itself be thin enough to look watery.

Slip trailing (L)

A slip trailer can be bought; or you can make one yourself from a feather quill, a cork and a rubber tube. Eye-droppers are best for small-scale work. Make sure the slip is trailed in a steady flow. This technique is most successful on flat surfaces. (9 to 12)

Slip combing and feathering

Slip is poured on to a flat leather-hard piece of clay; the surplus is drained off; lines are trailed across the wet surface in contrasting slips, and then these are dragged and patterned with a feather or the teeth of a cardboard 'comb'. (9 to 12)

Masking

Paper shapes are stuck over a leather-hard dish or relief to form a pattern, and slip is poured over the whole piece. When the slip is dry, the paper is peeled off, leaving its shapes behind in the colour of the underlying clay. This is a good follow-up to paint spraying with masks (see page 39). (9 to 12)

Sgraffito

This is the scratching of patterns with a sharp point into a dry layer of slip, to reveal the colour of the underlying clay. (9 to 12)

Incising

Decorations are cut into clay with a sharp point. (9 to 12)

Painting

Slip can be used with a brush on leather-hard clay as though it were creamy paint. (8 to 12)

Underglaze colours (or metal oxides mixed with a very little Polycell) can also be painted on to biscuit ware and then glazed with a transparent glaze. (9 to 12)

Relief decoration

The leather-hard surface is cut away or built up to make a design. When clay is soft it can be pinched into ridges. (9 to 12)

Impressing (L)

Designs are made by pressing objects into soft or leather-hard clay; which relates closely to printing on paper (see pages 43-45). (8 to 12)

Texturing

Many different things are used to texture the responsive surface of clay. These are some of the more promising: muslin, a meat-beater, pieces of tyre, tree-bark, the rough side of hardboard, a broken half-brick, a texturing wheel, hessian, rough sacking. Up to a point, the softer the clay, the more readily it will take a surface, but beware of trying to texture soggy pots. Hair-like deposits are produced when soft clay is pushed through a sieve; and broken pieces of coloured glass, iron filings or aluminium swarf also offer possibilities.

Glass

At least 1,040 °C is required for melting most kinds of glass adequately, and some have to be taken higher. Glass fired to stoneware temperature (above 1,200 °C) has a clear and crystal look, but few primary schools possess stoneware kilns. Glass always comes out crazed from a firing.

These are all good for experimenting with: the old type of red reflector or rear-light, discarded fragments of stained glass, marbles, glass beads, and green, blue or brown bottle glass. The size of the pieces depends on what is being made; be sure that glass is broken carefully, inside a tough bag, using a hammer. And be very careful to avoid 'frozen cataracts' of molten glass in the kiln. (Careful children from 10 to 12)

Body-stains

These are wedged into clay to colour it all the way through. This becomes expensive when more than a small amount of clay is used. (10 to 12)

Pigments

As pigments are made of stains (metal oxides) and water only, they can be laid on leather-hard or biscuit clay. Metal oxides can be used as slip-stains, body-stains, glaze-stains, and as underglaze colours. Podmore's 'Underglaze Colours' are suitable. (8 to 12)

FIRING

Schools without kilns often leave their clay-work in its natural state. To add colour to unfired clay, paint it first and then try rubbing it with a wax polish. Varnish tends to give clay a meretricious sheen.

Biscuit

Unglazed pottery that has been fired once is called BISCUIT ware (it has a deceptive resemblance to Digestive biscuit) and many pieces are happily left in this condition. Sometimes a glaze is fired on a raw pot, which saves a second firing. But usually a glaze is applied to a piece only when it has been biscuited; after which it is put into the kiln a second time for what is called the glost firing.

The higher that biscuit is fired, the harder and the less porous it will become. Good results come from firing biscuit between 1,100 °C and 1,120 °C, and glost at about 1,050 °C (which necessitates glazes that mature at this temperature).

Glazes need to be mixed thickly when they are used with biscuit that has been fired to 1,100 °C or higher.

The bottom-front of a kiln is usually the coolest part, and a full kiln fires more slowly than a lightly packed one. During packing, remember to keep everything at least half an inch away from the elements.

All ware must be dry before it is put in the kiln, and the temperature should rise slowly in the early stages of firing. To allow steam and gases to escape, the top spy-hole should be left open, and the temperature held at about 250 °C until tests with a cold mirror or knife show that all the moisture has evaporated. At about 800 °C carbon and other substances burn off, after which the spy-hole should be sealed with a bung.

Temperature is measured with a pyrometer or cones (see page 76). When the right level is reached, the kiln is switched off and left to cool. To even up the temperature throughout the kiln, 'soak' it for about half-an-hour, which means turn the regulator back to hold the temperature steady at its highest point. To avoid *dunting* (breaking) and cracking, it is important to keep all the bungs in place until the temperature has fallen below 100° C. Only then is it really safe to open the door.

If any of the biscuit does come out cracked – and it will be extremely lucky if none of it does – fill the cracks with Wenger's Biscuit Stopping.

GLAZING

Glazes are the wet skins deposited on biscuit ware by dipping or pouring. When dry they are fired between roughly 960 °C and 1,150 °C with earthenware, and 1,200 °C and 1,300 °C with stoneware. In the case of earthenware pots, glazes are functional as well as decorative because they prevent porosity; and this holds significance for children who make plant pots and bowls for use at home. They can find out about the relative porosity of earthenware and stoneware for themselves by experiment.

A glaze is a form of glass whose main ingredients are silica, alumina and a flux. Silica produces silicates that provide the glassy element; alumina gives body and stability which prevent the glaze from running and dripping; and the flux brings down its melting point. Lead is one of the best earthenware fluxes, but it is only reasonably safe when used in the form of an insoluble FRIT, which is a flux that has been previously fired and powdered. Frits melt between 750° and 900° C. Podmore's P2241 Lead Bisilicate is good. Borax is another flux. Beware of dust on biscuit before glazing, and on dry glaze before firing.

In order to transfer the ingredients of a glaze in a thin film to a piece of biscuit, they have to be powdered and mixed with water. The result is the powdery grey or white skin which comes from dipping a pot in a bowl of glaze, and which looks so unlikely to become a glittering coloured surface.

Dipping is the best method of glazing, but when it is not possible to have sufficient glaze mixed up in a bucket or breadbin to take a pot, the glaze has to be poured instead.

To glaze by *pouring*, first tip the glaze (which should be thoroughly stirred) into the pot and out again. Clean any dribbles off the outside and place the pot upside down on two wooden rails laid across a bowl. Pour the glaze over the pot, and then quickly lift it off the rails and put it down the right way up on a table, where any bare spots can be deftly touched up with the fingertips. When the glaze skin has gone matt, which usually happens surprisingly quickly, clean off the base and foot.

Recipes

A glaze can never radically improve the form of a pot, but a significant glaze is capable of changing an ordinary pot into a beautiful one.

It is wise to keep recipes for glazes as simple as possible, and to measure everything carefully, never adding 'pinches' of this or that. Always weigh the ingredients out dry, and add the water afterwards. Stir the mixture thoroughly and then brush it through 40-mesh, 80-mesh and 120-mesh sieves.

Children need to know, in simple terms, what is doing what in the mixtures they prepare; and whenever they produce a new glaze they must test it on test-tiles or test-pots before they make up a full batch. When you are following the more practical (cyclic) approach, the children will use local materials as far as possible, and experiment with them in varying ways: Will paint colour a glaze? If not, why not? What will iron filings do to a glaze?

It is possible to make stoneware glazes, in which wood ash acts as the flux, entirely from local materials; but with earthenware glazes a commercial frit is necessary. Here is a basic recipe to experiment with:

P2241 Lead Bisilicate: about 50 parts .(Podmore)
Local clay or river mud: about 50 parts.

Stains and other materials can be added to colour this and to modify it variously. It is likely to mature between 980° and 1,080 °C.

Up to 10 per cent of metal oxides can be added to glazes without their metallic quality predominating. Bentonite or sugar will prevent glazes from settling unstirrably, and sugar or Polycell helps to ensure that a glaze will stick uniformly to biscuit without cracking or coming away. Five to ten per cent of whiting mats a glaze. Here are some basic earthenware glazes used at Loughborough College of Art:

A white glaze (maturing at 1,050 °C)
P2241 Lead Bisilicate: 4 lbs 8 ozs
China Clay: 1 lb 3½ ozs
Flint or Quartz: 4½ ozs
Tin Oxide: 12 ozs

A transparent glaze (maturing at 1,050 °C)
  P2241 Lead Bisilicate: 4 lbs 11 ozs
       Ball Clay: 1 lb 4 ozs
       Flint or Quartz: 7 ozs
Clear honey (maturing at 1,050 °C)
  P2241 Lead Bisilicate: 4 lbs 11 ozs
  Ball Clay (or local clay): 1 lb 4 ozs
  Quartz: 5 ozs
  Red Iron Oxide: 1 oz
  Manganese Oxide: $1\frac{1}{2}$ ozs
A black glaze (maturing at 1,050 °C)
  P2241 Lead Bisilicate: 4 lbs 11 ozs
  Ball Clay (or local clay): 1 lb 4 ozs
  Quartz: 5 ozs
  Red Iron Oxide: 2 ozs
  Manganese Oxide: $4\frac{1}{2}$ ozs
  Cobalt Carbonate: $\frac{3}{4}$ oz

All these ingredients are supplied by Podmore.

Here are four possible ways of completing a pot:

1. Dip red terra-cotta biscuit in black glaze and decorate the surface with white glaze trailed from a slip trailer.
2. A pot that has been dabbed, when leather-hard, with white slip and coppery slip, is dried, fired to biscuit and then glazed with transparent glaze.
3. A leather-hard terra-cotta body is dabbed with coppery slip, dried, biscuited and glazed with honey glaze.
4. Terra-cotta biscuit is dipped in thin white glaze. A design is incised on this as soon as the glaze is mat, and then the pot is dipped in clear honey, within three-quarters of an hour.

Glaze faults

Crawling (bare patches are left in the glaze). Possible causes and cures:

1. The glaze was cracked before firing – Add Polycell or sugar to the mix.
2. There was dust on the pot when the glaze was applied.
3. The glaze was too thick.

4. The glaze was under-fired.

5. The glaze was fired before it was dry.

6. The biscuit was too porous – Fire to a higher temperature.

Crazing (the glaze is cracked). Try firing the biscuit to a higher temperature, or adding flint to the glaze.

Blistering. Refire the piece.

Running and dripping. Add alumina in the form of ball clay or local clay.

A list of pottery suppliers

Acme Marls Ltd., Clough Street, Hanley, Stoke-on-Trent – for kiln furniture, bats and props.

Bricesco, 1 Park Avenue, Wolstanton, Newcastle, Staffordshire – for sieve brushes.

Dryad Handicrafts Ltd., Northgates, Leicester – for plasticine and Clayola.

Hartley Wood & Co., Portobello Glass Works, Monkwearmouth, Sunderland – for glass.

New Clay Products Ltd., Overston House, Sunnyfields Road, Chislehurst, Kent – for a new type of modelling clay.

Podmore & Sons Ltd., Caledonian Mills, Shelton, Stoke-on-Trent – for almost everything to do with pottery.

Potclays Ltd., Wharf House, Copeland Street, Stoke-on-Trent – for Ivanhoe Tile Clay.

Wenger Ltd., Etruria, Stoke-on-Trent – general suppliers.

NOTE

1. For some useful guidance, see Leach (44), page 190.

FURTHER READING

Here are seven books that offer a great variety of information about work with clay: Clark (16), Kenny (41), Leach (44), Nicol (57), Rhodes (68), Rottger (71), Ruscoe (74).

5 The Happy School

THE CLASSROOM ETHOS

In every classroom where teaching is taking place – teaching to which children are required by law to be subjected – there is an atmosphere, or ETHOS, created by the teacher. The quality of their learning is determined by the quality of this classroom ethos, which can vary greatly from school to school, and also between classrooms. Largely through the competent managing of relationships, a sound teacher is able to establish a successful learning ethos that encourages deep and satisfying education. Within this happy general ethos, and often contributing greatly to it, there will also be established a specific FORMATIVE ethos, connected with creative work.

Social activity is to do with the way in which people behave towards each other inside their environment. From the simple structure of the family, to complicated international organisations, human relationships are inextricably bound up with achievement or failure. Since bad relationships can poison enterprises in many ways both inside and outside school – through blocking initiative or discouraging ability, or through mistaken judgements or false decisions – the question of relationships in general is extremely important for anyone concerned with teaching, and indeed, with all kinds of social activity.

If men and women in authority are sensible, they never allow themselves to forget what it is like having to do something you do not want to do; and so they are tolerant and just, relying on persuasion rather than compulsion. And this applies to the teacher in relation to the class as much as the headteacher to the school. However suitable the school building, or sound the educational theory, or highly qualified the teacher, what matters most in a classroom is the way the teacher and the children behave towards each other, and towards their work together; that is, the classroom ethos. A teacher who can create a happy and buoyant atmosphere in which the children are busy because they want to be, through guidance, encouragement and inspiration – but rarely imposition – is clearly able to establish the essentials of a first-rate learning situation.

Of course, there is every kind of classroom ethos in this country, from the most authoritarian, in which relationships are usually built on fear, to the most permissive, in which nobody has a strong creative purpose and there is a feeling of dissatisfaction. Somewhere between these extremes there lies a desirable mean where the best learning situations are brought about by the happy interplay of many factors. Among these, *the children* (with special reference to their age and character), and *their teacher*, are the most obvious and important. Others include the administrative authorities such as education officers, the headteacher, other members of the school staff, the school building, the parents and the area in which the school stands.

TEACHER RELATIONSHIPS

There is only room here to touch on a few of the important points affecting the classroom ethos, but several books that deal significantly with the teacher's role are mentioned under 'Further Reading' at the end of this chapter; and others are listed in the Bibliography on pages 120-122 ff.

Teachers

If we are to have happier children, we must also have happier teachers. Whereas progressive educationists rightly stress how vital it is that children should be surrounded by everything likely to set their minds at ease, to reduce boredom, and to give them a sense of purpose, it is sometimes forgotten that precisely the same applies to teachers. After all, teachers and children belong to the same species, and if it is true to say of children that they work best when they have powerful motives for doing so, it is also true of teachers. A woman teacher who regards her work as only another way of earning her livelihood before marriage is no better motivated than a child who attends school because the government says he must.

Teachers, in order to be truly successful, need to be emotionally committed to their work. They need to feel it is worthwhile, and that they are really helping to shape the future – however unlikely that may sometimes seem – through their activities with the small, varied and sometimes exasperating people in their care. In this, their superiors can help greatly through positive and understanding attitudes. The best authorities, from the Education Secretary himself to the Local Education Authorities and head-teachers, are those who do everything possible to show that a teacher's services are not only desirable and welcome, but also vital to the continued health of our society. Teachers are as much subject to cynicism and frustration as other people, and there is a great deal that can be done to counter these feelings and strengthen purpose through in-service training, formative free periods, film shows, courses, teachers' centres, trips, recreation, and discussion groups.

Headteachers

There was once a headmaster who is reported to have stood at the door of his school with a stopwatch and time-book at ten minutes to nine every morning; and another who used to relate his allocation of materials to staff on the basis of 'attitude' – that is, if he thought a teacher's attitude was deteriorating, he would reduce her material allowance, and so penalise children for something of which they were innocent.

These are not examples of men who were positive in their relationships. The most successful modern headteachers are not only scrupulously fair (and, therefore, indifferent to their private likes and dislikes) but also careful to foster the *positive qualities* in the people they work with, by the recognition and encouragement of their potentialities for good, rather than by attempts to stamp out their faults.

And the same is true of the most successful class teachers. They will always need to work against the enjoyment of power and the temptation to have favourites.

G

People in authority who are capable of EMPATHY, meaning that they can sympathetically project themselves in their imagination into other people's situations, will not be able to enjoy wielding power over others for long. Democracy in a school is an inter-acting, mutually-reliant, creative pattern of relationships.

Headteachers who are able to gain the confidence and co-operation of their staff will usually find they are building a happy school.

The staff room

Some teachers find it easier to deal with children than with their colleagues on the staff. A few may even achieve good learning situations with the children in their classrooms while being withdrawn and silent, irascible, or even assertive, in the staff room. There is little doubt that such learning situations would be lifted from whatever level they may have reached if such teachers could bring themselves to enter into a spirit of co-operation and mutual respect with their colleagues; for a truly happy school partly depends on happy relationships among the staff. Most people who have taught for any length of time will have had experience of the inefficiency and damage to children's interests that can spring from prolonged confrontations in the staff room – amusing though these may sometimes be.

As always in matters of relationships, the answer lies in tolerance and respect: the best kind of community democracy exists where it is recognised that every individual possesses positive rather than negative qualities, and that these are the ones to concern us. Negative criticism is almost always destructive. It usually rises from envy or contempt or single-minded commitment to some system of ideas (it is almost as easy to be intolerant and committed as it is to be tolerant and uncommitted), but the balanced, creative person is both tolerant of others and enthusiastically devoted to his beliefs. We all tend to underestimate our colleagues.

The building

Although children rarely show much interest in their schools as buildings (it is usually their teachers or other children that interest them most), and although it is possible to create a first-rate learning situation in a leaky greenhouse and an equally poor one in a 'glass palace', few teachers would deny that a well-designed building makes for happier children and staff. If the building is light and harmoniously colourful, with an element of excitement about it which stirs the imagination, if it is spacious and convenient, and if you find balance, proportion and good taste wherever you go, then your spirits will naturally tend to rise when you come to school, even on the most grey and dreary mornings. The sense of being inside something harmonious and complete has a beneficial effect: sensitive teachers and children respond to it with the desire to behave and work creatively in ways that are correspondingly satisfying.

There has been a tendency in the past to regard the hall as the nucleus of a school, and so to build around it. But recently, as the accent on research and cross-reference by the children themselves has increased, the claims of the library to lie at the centre of school life have grown stronger. One design for a modern junior school puts a circular library in the middle of a ring of classrooms, which is in turn surrounded by a ring of activity areas. The level of noise will be highest in the activity areas at the periphery and lowest in the library at the centre (see figure, page 100).

Of course, whatever has been done by the architect can be enhanced by the children themselves through the display of their own work, bringing both a unique and changing character to the building, and a sense of it being lived and worked in. Children's work is unequalled for bringing vitality to a room or corridor.

There are also ways of quickly adapting a building for different uses. Teachers are able to alter dramatically the surroundings of their classes in those schools that have replaced traditional classrooms with large areas, which can be easily modified with screens, curtains or partitions. If clay work and other art activities are going to occupy a class in one of these schools, a number of relatively small cubicles are quickly established; when the time comes for mime, or running about, or singing, the cubicles are moved away to make an open space.

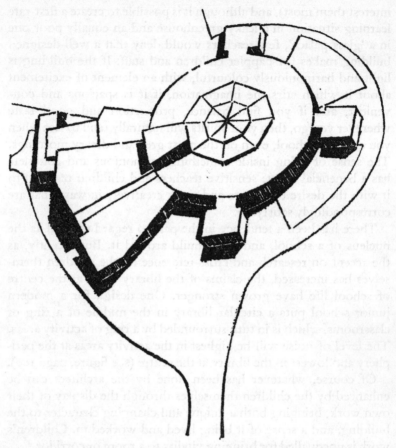

Thurmaston Round School. The library forms a nucleus to the teaching areas. Its walls are completely glazed, so that children in the bases can see the books.

THE FORMATIVE ETHOS

Progressive primary schools no longer divide each day into watertight compartments labelled 'mathematics', 'English' or 'art'. With the use of assignments, topics, themes and general 'activity methods', almost all lessons become experiences in learning about life, rather than studies of particular 'subjects'. Indeed, it is possible for a single lesson to cover several of the old subjects at once. However, good sense often requires teachers

Plate 17. *Trawlers* 21″ × 27″. (Two girls – 9½ years.) A rich pattern of felt triangles, suggested by sails. The large flat shapes are relieved and partly repeated by the thin linear triangles.

Plate 18. *Mobile Arms: 2′ Total height: about 6′* (Girl – 16 years.)
Three 'storeys' can sometimes be too many for children of
middle-school age.

to limit some lessons to a minimum of practical activity, and to bias others towards it. Whenever children are engaged on practical work in a happy school a certain easily recognised atmosphere is generated, which nourishes creativity, and contributes significantly to the general ethos. In any classroom where such a *formative ethos* has developed, there is a gentle buzz of busy noise, the children move about only on essential errands, and the teacher becomes a source of inspiration and encouragement rather than of direction. This is the best kind of discipline: the self-imposed communal discipline of enthusiastic absorption which no teacher achieves always, but at which every teacher should aim. (A formative ethos can, of course, be developed in many ways that are not 'artistic' within the limited sense of 'art' work; for example, through writing stories and poems.)

Planning for practical activities

In order to reach a formative ethos based on practical activities with a class, it is first essential to plan carefully and to make sure that all the necessary materials and equipment are intelligently placed around the room. A classroom specially designed for practical work will clearly be relatively easy to adapt to particular needs; and yet, even in a room without water it is possible to carry on successful practical lessons.

Here are some points to consider when planning practical activity in a traditionally-designed classroom, which lacks benches and activity areas:

1. With the children, decide on the number of groups best suited to the work in hand, and arrange the desks or tables accordingly.
2. Use monitors to help to distribute materials and equipment, such as paper, brushes, paint and water (in big plastic mugs or containers).
3. If there is no sink, put at least two buckets in an accessible position on the floor: one for clean water and the other for dirty water.
4. If there is a sink, make certain that there is a clear path leading to it. (Free-standing sinks are valuable.)

5. Prepare a special area for materials likely to make a mess, such as clay. An old table is useful for working on; and you may need to cover the floor under it with polythene or newspapers.

6. Distribute and arrange your learning aids, such as lengths of fabric, pieces of stone, fresh herrings or a wall chart. (If your classroom is near a fish tank or a conservatory you will have valuable learning aids permanently available.)

7. Keep a space ready on the wall for display.

8. Use your monitors at the end to help with the clearing up (which they usually enjoy).

9. Try to reach a balance between planned looking ahead and spontaneous alterations to plans, which arise from the children's activity.

10. It is useful to have some way of blacking out windows for projection. I have found venetian blinds the most versatile, since they can be sensitively adjusted to your requirements – but they are sometimes awkward when very long.

Ideally, the display areas should include a stretch of peg-board for small models and collages, the store-room should be about one fifth of the total classroom area, the floor easy to wash, the sinks fitted with silt traps, and there should be a covered terrace or verandah for working on during the summer. But few schools are equipped with all these amenities, and usually a teacher is forced to adapt whatever exists to whatever she wants.

Cleanliness

There was once a student who was taking an art lesson with some nine-year-olds, when the headmaster came in and looked critically around the room. Suddenly he stooped, picked up a single piece of charcoal and said in a loud voice, 'Mr Cadwallader, I don't care what you do with these children during the periods you are foisted upon them, *but you're not making a mess of my school floor!*'

This is a clear-cut example of the belief among some head-teachers that cleanliness is more important than creativity. Though it is easy to sympathise with one side of this view – after all, society has entrusted them with a building costing a great deal, and they are justly proud – little sound formative work can take place in a room that is treated like a ward in a hospital. In fact, I always think that if a classroom looks very clean and tidy – if it has an un-lived in look – then there is something wrong. The sensible headteacher is never worried by a few splashes of paint around the sink, or a mark or two on the desks, so long as these are honourable scars; and the sensible class teacher balances consideration for the cleaners responsible for the classroom with the reasonable demands of energetic children.

Folders and exhibitions

If each child in a school has a folder, which he keeps throughout his school career for his two-dimensional work, he will gain a sense of gradually increasing achievement; and also his teachers will be able to see how he is developing. Every now and again, selections can be taken from these folders and small exhibitions arranged. It is possible to mount other exhibitions from objects brought in by children following class themes. 'Red Things', 'Bright Things' or 'Art and Science' offer possibilities.

Children like to see whatever they have made or brought displayed around their school. It gives them a sense of achievement and of being part of the community ('Look, mum, sir's put up my porcupine!').

In general, because process-exhibitions are more valuable than end-product exhibitions, it is better to display too much than too little. An overcrowded classroom exhibition, representative of the whole class, has more value for the children than a tasteful arrangement of selected pieces of work done by a few art stars. A small backward boy does not feel encouraged to do 'even better next time' when he finds that his painting has not been put up.

And yet sometimes selection must take place. Adults usually want to exhibit end-products; it is important to keep a close check on this aspect of work, and make a conscious effort to empathise with the viewpoint of the child. It is not easy for an adult to look more at processes than at finished work when considering works of art – and moreover, *to look at them from the child's angle*. Yet this is what the sensible teacher must do. Never, therefore, hesitate to put up something because it is unfinished.

The moment we display a piece of work we establish a standard – 'Sir's put it up, so he must like it'. And this standard will influence the children whether we want it to or not. Therefore, we need to ask ourselves certain questions when arranging a display, in order to form our criteria. The most important points are these:

How will exhibiting this piece of work affect the child who did it? Will it encourage him to go further, or will it make him think he can always gain success by repeating this type of thing? (We want work that shows growth and encourages further growth.)

Has he been honest in what he has done here? That is, has he been true to himself?

Is he finding himself here, or is he just copying something wrong for him?

What does this piece of work communicate? Not so much to me, the adult, as to children? How will it affect *them*? Does it enlarge *their* experience? Has it qualities of energy, feeling or imagination that *they* can appreciate?

Then – will it enhance the classroom ethos?

These are more important points than the *esoteric-aesthetic* points from the world of adult standards that are raised so often (see also 'Assessment' on page 28).

In general, it is best to encourage children to make their own displays and to do their own lettering. For this, big pieces of charcoal are useful, and square-ended lettering chalk, italic pens, flat brushes, or even 'pens' made from rectangles of cardboard and used with Brusho colours. Try to introduce the elements of poster design with the older children, remembering margins, a happy balance between blocks of lettering and other motifs, legibility and the selection of what is significant. Spraying with inks around a lettered mask is a successful means of producing headings like 'CLASS TWO: RETROSPECTIVE EXHIBITION'. Colourful letters cut from card, and laid on a neutral background, have power.

With its concealed lighting illuminating three-dimensional

work, a Visual Music Box (see page 49) establishes an excellent centre-piece to an exhibition.

Trellis work, bought from a gardening shop, can be quickly rigged up for vertical display, and the eye can be led pleasingly below and around it over varied levels and surfaces made from tables, stools and chairs. Blocks of wood are useful for raising exhibits, and so are bricks or breeze blocks that have been painted white. A circle of sand or gravel placed around a pot or a small model will help to focus attention on it.

Whereas it is sufficient for quick classroom displays to put work up with nothing more elaborate than mapping pins or painted drawing pins, anything for more permanent display needs to be properly framed and hung. For this, it is wise to keep a dozen or more frames of the same size as the paper used in school. But remember that displays, exhibitions, and individual pieces of work, lose their appeal for the children quickly, and even the most attractive should be changed after a few weeks.

If a school is able to join a picture loan service it will always have a small selection of good adult work on the walls; and if some of this has been painted by artists living locally the children will see that art of a high standard is being produced there and and then in places that they know.

When children's work is generously exhibited at vantage points around a school, the beneficent effects of successful lessons inside individual classrooms are brought to influence the ethos of the whole building, so that it becomes possible to talk about *a formative school ethos* which enfolds everyone, and which is stimulating to many different kinds of creativity.

SUMMARY

Good relationships between a teacher, the class and their work bring about a happy classroom ethos or atmosphere, which is decisive in establishing a sound learning situation. Other factors also bear on this. A formative ethos, springing from creative activity within a happy classroom ethos, favourably affects the overall ethos of a school. Sound relationships depend largely on tolerance and empathy. Points about planning and displaying.

FURTHER READING

The teacher's role is well dealt with in these books: Hughes and Hughes (35), chapter xviii; Langford (43), chapters 8 and 9; Musgrave (56), chapter 5. Mock (55) is readable and perceptive about teaching art in schools. Marshall (51) describes a successful and stimulating experiment in establishing a good learning situation and a formative ethos. Brown and Precious (12) describe integration in their own schools.

6 Schemes and Themes

During each of your three years of training you will go into a school for a period of observation and practical teaching. However surprised you may be during these 'Practices' at the difference between your expectations and the reality, you will be wise to accept and adapt to the established customs of each school you enter. Not only will you have to be sensitive to the methods of the headteacher and to the school generally, but also to the methods of the class teacher you find yourself with, and the college lecturer who comes to see how you are getting on. This sometimes asks for a delicate sense of balance, and you will need to think and plan with all of them in mind.

It may be that art and other activities are taught for only a short fixed period in each week; or even that art is ignored altogether. On the other hand, the school may be run on integrated lines.

Are there any general principles that can help a student to meet the varied situations in which she may find herself?

Although there is no golden key, here are certain basic guidelines capable of general application:

1. Every lesson needs learning aids.
2. Be in your room in good time to prepare and arrange.
3. It is a mistake to begin with too many groups. Although an experienced teacher is able to keep in touch with at least half a dozen groups at a time, a student needs exceptional ability to run more than three or four different activities successfully at once.
4. Do not talk to a class for too long. Ten minutes is usually enough for inspiring interest that leads into activity.

5. The teacher must always be in charge, helping the children in the required direction.

6. The teacher must be firm, just and tolerant.

7. Remember that the tone of voice is the instrument with which to modulate the class, and establish workable relationships.

8. The teacher should not allow anti-social behaviour. It is when a child becomes a nuisance to someone else that restraint is necessary.

9. Many students tend to be too gentle with children through fear of not being liked. In a family, a loved mother or father is kindly but firm.

10. Do not make a threat without being prepared to carry it out.

11. There is an important difference between 'busy noise' and 'noisy noise'. 'Busyness' nearly always means happiness without disorder.

12. Lecturers often ask for notes about lessons. Different lecturers favour different kinds of notes. Try to adapt your notes both to the situation (see next section) and the lecturer.

13. Whenever you are critical, make sure that you are positive, too. Try to show each child his particular road ahead.

14. When a group or an individual has finished a piece of work, be ready with something else that is fresh and interesting.

15. The immediate goal remains the best possible learning situation.

Lesson notes

Since, in a properly interwoven syllabus, the children's activity in a class will lead anywhere that you consider rewarding, a general guide (full of starting points and links and open to modification) is more realistic than a fixed plan. However, if the time-table you are given is a traditional one, you may be asked to prepare traditional notes showing an aim for each lesson, and how you mean to introduce, develop and conclude it – with the conclusions that you draw from it, too, when you reflect on what happened in the lesson itself.

In a more flexible time-table situation, a day-by-day diary helps

Above: – Plate 19. *The Cow Jumped Over the Moon. About* 3′ × 4′. (Group work – 8 and 9 years.) Shadow puppets. Main materials: two bright bulbs, black card on sticks, and a sheet stretched on a wooden frame.

Below: – Plate 20. *Circles* 9″. (Boy – 11 years.) A mosaic made from sand, barley, lentils and broken eggshells, stuck on to paper.

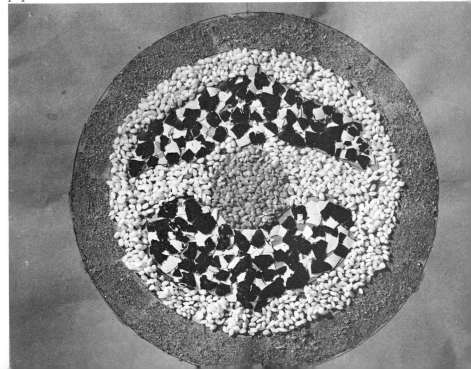

Plate 21. *Goose* 28″ × 40″ × 28″. (Group work – remedial children – 8 to 11 years.) Papier mâché and metal foil over a wire frame. A piece like this helps children to learn how to work together imaginatively.

Plate 22. *Three Masks, each about 6″ × 8″.* (Boys – 11 years.) Papier mâché, painted and varnished. Round elastic at the back enables the masks to be worn.

to bring your ideas together into a form that both shows your tutor how you are progressing and enables you to evaluate your own achievements.

Unlike adults, children rarely choose to remain seated for long (just as they rarely walk like adults, preferring to 'walk wobbly', or to run or walk backwards, or to hop or skip). For this reason, they are happier and more at ease when they are able to move about on valid assignments for at least part of their time in class. Small cards, called 'assignment' (or 'task') cards make useful starters. They can be written out very quickly by the teacher in order to focus and question: for example, 'How long is the fish tank?' 'What is the temperature in the room today?' 'Will your drawing change into a collage?' Small challenges of this kind can become part of a lasting treasure-hunt.

In any lesson-guide that is prepared, the starters and theme will form most of what is planned and definite in the teacher's mind, whereas the rest of the lesson will be comparatively indefinite, taking shape only as the children work. Nevertheless, in drawing up a guide it is wise to plot the *probable* course of the lesson, and the *probable* materials needed for it, or else the indefinite will soon become the disorderly. If themes and starters that have exhilarating meanings for the children themselves are selected, this will avoid the artificiality that comes from imposed projects.

Here are some extracts from the hypothetical guide-and-diary of an ambitious student, which relate to a school where daily assignments in reading, writing and arithmetic are followed by Topic Work. The school is moving towards 'Integration'. Thirty-five eight-and nine-year-olds are divided into groups for the assignments, which are written out on cards by the student and class teacher, and recorded with coloured pegs on a board (and also in a book) as soon as they are completed. (Because a teacher must ensure that whatever individuals are good at is balanced with whatever they are weak in, some records are indispensable. In art classes, children may record their achievements in decorated lists, which are themselves artefacts.)

The student has told the class about a Stately Home that has collected a zoo to stave off bankruptcy. Although her style leaves something to be desired, her expression is direct and fluent. The class teacher is helping her with the six or seven groups she has accumulated.

Tuesday, 8th October

As soon as the assignments are finished we want to carry on with our Zoo theme. Trishia and Bobby are writing their poems about the polar bear who escaped and ended up in the village hairdresser's. This probably won't take them too long, and I expect they will then start painting it. The six at the clay table are meaning to try and finish their models of the animals and the Duke and Duchess. The big group on the collage have a long way to go. They are still so disappointingly *stolid* in their use of colours and materials. We *must* try and guide them into thinking more adventurously. The story writers are likely to go on working for over an hour, but when they begin to flag we mean to bring them into the group making the big map of the park, showing all the animal and visitor amenities. (Dare I try introducing *area* on this map in a few days?)

Herbie Bostock is likely to go on working away at his mosaic under Miss Heath's table, and as long as it keeps going the way it's going now we're not going to stop him.

Ideas for the future: A shadow puppet play by a group – could the Duchess be swallowed by the hippo? Last week, the ship which brought the animals from Africa led to an exciting model made from scraps. Can I use this for the Time-and-Distance, or for *The Development of the Ship*, later on? (They were asking about paddle steamers.) I want them to do more *research* from *books* . . .

Needed today: Paints; brushes; paper; clay; newspapers; aprons; scissors; fabrics; Marvin Medium; charcoal; map; inks; magazines; bucket of Polycell.

(Later) Forgot the Vicar was coming in to give one of his talks, so we didn't get nearly as far as we'd hoped. However, the poems were good. I liked Trishias specially:

> '. . . All the ladies looked up and saw,
> His long white nose around the door. . . .'

Some of the clay models were vigorous, but I'm still very disappointed about the collage people, and the story writers never finished – though I suppose it doesn't really matter. Herbie Bostock happy under the table. . . .

Wednesday, 9th October

Finish stories and start map. The clay modellers are still keen, and I think we may try 'slipping' some of the models today. They're talking about a large panorama model, rather like the map, but in clay . . .

(Later) Foiled again! First of all, cascades of water in the staff-room from a burst pipe, and then the heating system conked out at 2 and we had to send them all home early. It was *freezing*!

Friday, 11th October

Progressing well. Several collage and story people have formed new group writing shadow puppet play. This afternoon, everyone so interested in the barn which blew down up at the farm that I agreed to let anyone paint, write or draw about the barn – and some of the results were *marvellous*! You could have heard an ink drop. Miss Heath very pleased. We have decided that Herbie's mosaic, though good, is definitely finished now. . . .

Tuesday, 15th October

Clay models all finished and nearly dry. We're going to fire them next Monday I hope. The panorama has turned out *bitty*, and we've had some cracking. Now the collage is finished I think this group has used up their part of the theme, and I'm going to start them on big clay prints of ideas in the collage which look promising. We mean to do a bit of swopping between groups. The playwrights have invented a fire in the Duke's gun room which is spreading rapidly. – *But in shadow puppets*! – I think I may have to throw cold water on this. (Miss Heath is doubtful about it, too.) I liked the way Petula represented the Duchess inside the Hippo, with pink and blue tissue paper (shadow puppets). We have done some research on ship development, and Bobby has got some good ideas. Area has begun to work out well – at present they are cutting out simple shapes for measuring. Herbie's just beginning to join in with the others at last.

Needed: Hardish slabs of clay for clay prints. Impressing and incising tools. Sheet and frame for shadow puppets. Scissors. . . .

Teacher and child

A few children respond so readily to creative activity that once they have found themselves in a warm and formative classroom ethos, they need very little help. Most children, however, are not able to realise their visions and capabilities (or, indeed, to have visions at all) without a teacher's persuasion and encouragement.

In the following piece of dialogue, I have tried to show several ways in which a teacher can extend the feeling and thinking of a diffident child by patiently questioning and suggesting.

The boy, who is nine, has decided to paint a picture of a stone-age family by their cave; but so far has done very little.

Teacher: Hullo, Gilbert, how are you doing? (Gilbert makes an indefinite noise.) Well, I like your start with the rocks, anyway. . . Still, are you sure that's all you can do?

Gilbert: Can't paint people . . . (*pause*).

Teacher: I'm not so sure . . . What would you *like* to paint, then?

Gilbert: (after another pause): Dunno, really. . . .

Teacher: Didn't the story do anything to you, Gilbert?

Gilbert: Eh?

Teacher: Didn't the story *say* anything to you? – I mean, did it give you any ideas? . . . Didn't it make you *think* about anything or *feel* anything you wanted to paint, Gilbert?

Gilbert: Dunno, really. . .

Marlene: It did *me*, Miss Cadmium!

Ingrid: And *me*, too, Miss! – It did me!

Miss Cadmium: Shhh! – Yes, you two are doing very well. But everybody can't have good ideas about the same thing. Gilbert, I want you to listen to me carefully now – close your eyes and listen. Do you remember. . . They were all so very hungry – walking about all hungry and bent over? And everybody was very thin, like bent broomsticks, and the father went out into the forest every day with his two big sons and found nothing? All the leaves had fallen off the trees, remember? The branches looked very sharp and shrivelled, and there was bright, cold snow. . . One day . . . (She goes on for a little longer; and then she asks about different viewpoints: Should the picture be a close-up of the father stalking a deer? Or a crow's-eye view of the forest clearing? Or perhaps a general view of everybody roasting the rhino? Suddenly Gilbert seems to have an idea, and she leaves him. Ten minutes later, she comes back and finds that Gilbert has in front of him the beginnings of what is, for him, an expressive painting, with a late-evening feel about it. But Gilbert is beginning to flag. Should she suggest he finishes now and joins another group, or should she try once more? She senses that he would gain self respect by going on for a little longer, so she describes a stone-age family around their cave, again. There were wild beasts outside in the firelight.) . . . the animals' eyes made a pattern . . . like a string of fairy lights – Can you see them, Gilbert?

Gilbert: Yes, Miss – I think so, Miss. Can I start again, Miss?

Miss Cadmium: Yes, if you want to. Which paper would you like? (Gilbert chooses a dark sheet, and when Miss Cadmium comes back she is pleasantly surprised. And he said he couldn't paint people! After complimenting him, she decides to try to extend his ideas a little further by asking a few questions: 'Are there any people nearer the cave?'; 'Can you actually *see* any bears?'; 'What colours are there in a fire?' She leaves him alone until a few minutes later he has stopped again.) Gilbert, that's really very nice, you know! – Finished? – Stand over here and take a look . . . Well — is it?

Gilbert: No Miss, don't reckon so.

Miss Cadmium: Oh? . . . *Well* then . . . ?

Gilbert: It don't seem quite finished somehow, Miss . . . Dunno, quite . . .

Miss Cadmium: All right . . . What about the *darkness*, Gilbert? – The feeling of all being round a fire there, depending on each other for everything . . . Try to see it in your mind, if you can . . . (In the end, Gilbert paints a picture that is more imaginative and inventive than anything he has done before. Miss Cadmium pins it up, and Gilbert joins a group making a collage. Later, in reviewing some recent work, Miss Cadmium asks Gilbert several questions in front of the whole class: Can he remember exactly how he mixed his blackish greens? What made him think of that pattern of gleaming

H

A TOWN LIKE OURS

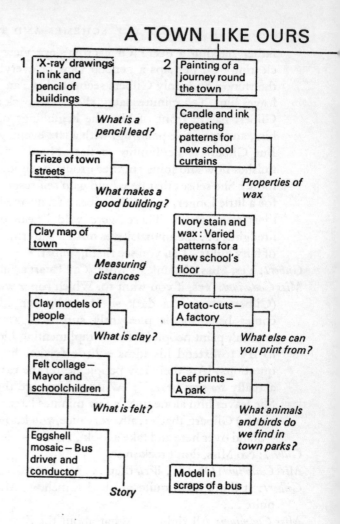

1

'X-ray' drawings in ink and pencil of buildings

What is a pencil lead?

Frieze of town streets

What makes a good building?

Clay map of town

Measuring distances

Clay models of people

What is clay?

Felt collage — Mayor and schoolchildren

What is felt?

Eggshell mosaic — Bus driver and conductor

Story

2

Painting of a journey round the town

Candle and ink repeating patterns for new school curtains

Properties of wax

Ivory stain and wax : Varied patterns for a new school's floor

Potato-cuts — A factory

What else can you print from?

Leaf prints — A park

What animals and birds do we find in town parks?

Model in scraps of a bus

**A TOWN
LIKE OURS
Eight and nine
year olds**

Eight and nine year olds

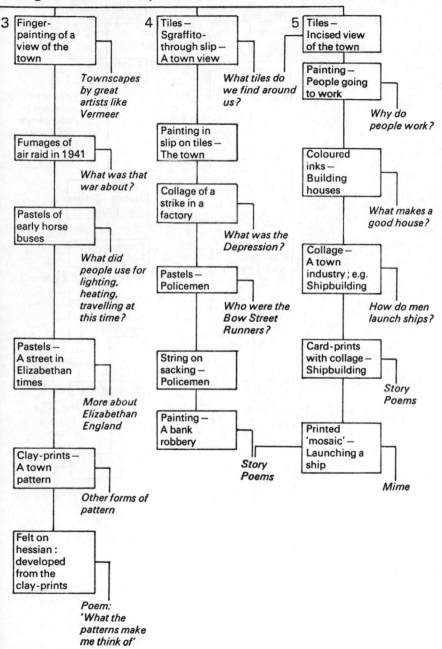

3 Finger-painting of a view of the town

Townscapes by great artists like Vermeer

Fumages of air raid in 1941

What was that war about?

Pastels of early horse buses

What did people use for lighting, heating, travelling at this time?

Pastels — A street in Elizabethan times

More about Elizabethan England

Clay-prints — A town pattern

Other forms of pattern

Felt on hessian: developed from the clay-prints

Poem: 'What the patterns make me think of'

4 Tiles — Sgraffito-through slip — A town view

What tiles do we find around us?

Painting in slip on tiles — The town

Collage of a strike in a factory

What was the Depression?

Pastels — Policemen

Who were the Bow Street Runners?

String on sacking — Policemen

Painting — A bank robbery

Story Poems

5 Tiles — Incised view of the town

Painting — People going to work

Why do people work?

Coloured inks — Building houses

What makes a good house?

Collage — A town industry; e.g. Shipbuilding

How do men launch ships?

Card-prints with collage — Shipbuilding

Story Poems

Printed 'mosaic' — Launching a ship

Mime

THE SEA

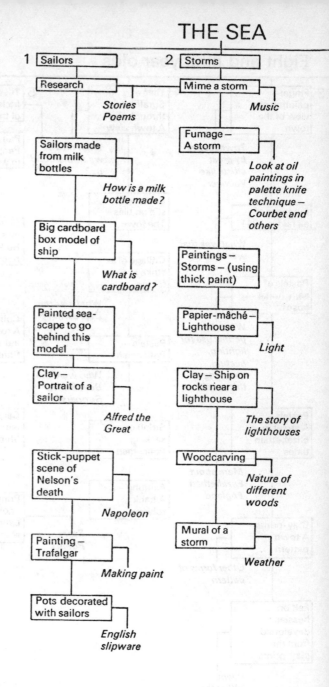

1 Sailors
— Research

*Stories
Poems*

Sailors made
from milk
bottles

*How is a milk
bottle made?*

Big cardboard
box model of
ship

*What is
cardboard?*

Painted sea-
scape to go
behind this
model

Clay —
Portrait of a
sailor

*Alfred the
Great*

Stick-puppet
scene of
Nelson's
death

Napoleon

Painting —
Trafalgar

Making paint

Pots decorated
with sailors

*English
slipware*

2 Storms
— Mime a storm

Music

Fumage —
A storm

*Look at oil
paintings in
palette knife
technique —
Courbet and
others*

Paintings —
Storms — (using
thick paint)

Papier-mâché —
Lighthouse

Light

Clay — Ship on
rocks near a
lighthouse

*The story of
lighthouses*

Woodcarving

*Nature of
different
woods*

Mural of a
storm

Weather

THE SEA
Ten to twelve
year olds

Ten to twelve year olds

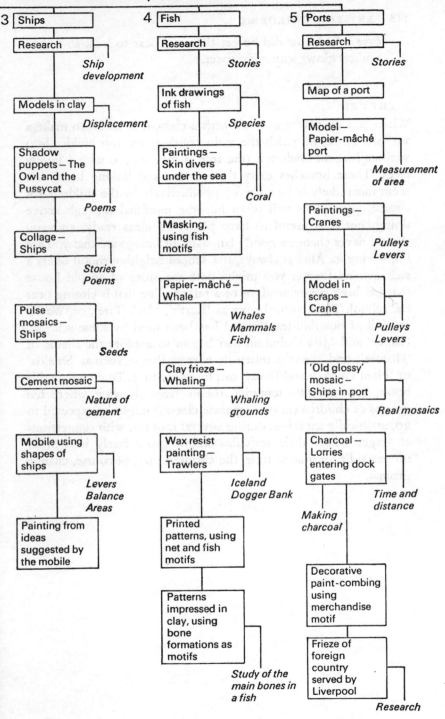

3 Ships
- Research
  - *Ship development*
- Models in clay
  - *Displacement*
- Shadow puppets – The Owl and the Pussycat
  - *Poems*
- Collage – Ships
  - *Stories Poems*
- Pulse mosaics – Ships
  - *Seeds*
- Cement mosaic
  - *Nature of cement*
- Mobile using shapes of ships
  - *Levers Balance Areas*
- Painting from ideas suggested by the mobile

4 Fish
- Research
  - *Stories*
- Ink drawings of fish
  - *Species*
- Paintings – Skin divers under the sea
  - *Coral*
- Masking, using fish motifs
- Papier-mâché – Whale
  - *Whales Mammals Fish*
- Clay frieze – Whaling
  - *Whaling grounds*
- Wax resist painting – Trawlers
  - *Iceland Dogger Bank*
- Printed patterns, using net and fish motifs
- Patterns impressed in clay, using bone formations as motifs
  - *Study of the main bones in a fish*

5 Ports
- Research
  - *Stories*
- Map of a port
- Model – Papier-mâché port
  - *Measurement of area*
- Paintings – Cranes
  - *Pulleys Levers*
- Model in scraps – Crane
  - *Pulleys Levers*
- 'Old glossy' mosaic – Ships in port
  - *Real mosaics*
- Charcoal – Lorries entering dock gates
  - *Making charcoal*
  - *Time and distance*
- Decorative paint-combing using merchandise motif
- Frieze of foreign country served by Liverpool
  - *Research*

eyes? And how did he get the cave bear to look so huge? Gilbert glows with self respect.)

THEMES

When you are planning work with a class, it is useful to make a THEME TREE, in which the main trunk at the top divides into various branches below it (the tree is inverted, as with a family tree). These branches carry the starters and linking ideas that seem most likely to be taken up productively by the children. Of course, your plans will often become modified through active doing, but it is useful to have plenty of ideas ready, and you should never change a good plan without being sure that you are improving it. Almost always, the school neighbourhood offers a rich general theme; you might take the story of an old house that has been condemned, or of a railway line that is closing near the school. Then, such themes as 'Earth', 'Air', 'Fire', or 'Water' are full of possibilities. 'Flight' has been used by some schools. Gilbert and Miss Cadmium had begun to explore the theme of 'Homes'; and even the relatively narrow theme, such as 'Shields' or 'Plant Growth and Decay' can be rewarding. To complete this book, here are two tentative theme trees showing where ten groups of children (in two separate classes) might be expected to go, artistically speaking, during several months, with suggestions at stages where their activities might grow freely into other interests. From time to time, the children may, of course, change groups.

FURTHER READING

During teaching practice it is very useful to have books that contain plenty of starting points in the classroom with you. Here is a brief selection from a field of hundreds.

Some books in the Ladybird Series are helpful, including *Heath and Woodland Birds* (46), *Pond Life* (78), *Lighthouses* (66) and *The Night Sky* (13). Bettini (9) and Grabar (28) clearly show the tesserae in the real mosaics they reproduce. Postma (63) and Shaw (79) offer starting points in plant structure. D'Arbelloff (21) and Hils (30) will give you many ideas; and so – in different ways – will *The Children's Picture Atlas* (15) and Bauchot (7).

Other books that contain starting points are listed in the Bibliography.

Bibliography

'S' against a book shows that it offers interesting starters for children.

S. 1. Anderson, Margaret *Through the Microscope* (Aldus 1965)

2. Arnheim, Rudolf *Towards a Psychology of Art* (Faber 1967)

3. Ash, Beryl & Rapaport, Barbara *Creative Work in the Junior School* (Methuen 1957)

S. 4. Bager, D. *Nature as Designer* (Warne 1967)

5. Bantock, G. H. *Freedom and Authority in Education* (Faber 1952)

6. Barney, W. D. *A Study of Perception and its relation to the Art Expression of a Group of Adolescents* (thesis) (University of London Institute of Education 1952)

S. 7. Bauchot, R. & M-L. *Album of Exotic Fish* (Elek 1964)

8. Berenson, Bernard *The Italian Painters of the Renaissance* (Phaidon 1952)

S. 9. Bettini, S. *I Mosaici di San Vitale a Ravenna* (Skira 1965)

10. Blackie, John *Inside the Primary School* (HMSO 1967)

S. 11. Braithwaite, D. *Fairground Architecture* (Evelyn 1968)

12. Brown, Mary & Precious, Norman. *The Integrated Day in the Primary School* (Ward Lock 1968)

S. 13. Brück, Mary *Ladybird: The Night Sky* (Wills & Hepworth 1965)

14. Catty, N. *Learning and Teaching in the Junior School* (Methuen 1956)

S. 15. *The Children's Picture Atlas* (Paul Hamlyn 1965)

16. Clark, Kenneth *Practical Pottery and Ceramics* (Studio Vista 1965)

S. 17. Clayton, Keith *The Earth's Crust* (Aldus 1967)

18. Collingwood, R. G. *The Principles of Art* (Oxford University Press 1938)

19. Compton, M. *Optical and Kinetic Art* (Tate Gallery 1967)

S. 20. Croy, O. R. *Creative Photo Micrography* (Focal Press 1968)

S. 21. d'Arbelloff, N. *Creating in Collage* (Studio Vista 1967)

S. 22. Déribéré, M. *Belles Roches, Beaux Cristaux* (Larousse 1956)

23. Dimmack, Max *A Dictionary of Creative Activities for Schools' Use* (Macmillan 1966)

24. Farr, Dennis *British Sculpture since 1945* (Tate Gallery 1965)

25. Garforth, F. W. *Education and Social Purpose* (Oldbourne 1962)
26. Gombrich, E. H. *Meditations on a Hobby Horse* (Phaidon 1965)
27. Gombrich, E. H. *The Story of Art* (Phaidon 1966)
S. 28. Grabar, André *Greek Mosaics of the Byzantine Period* (Collins/ Unesco 1964)
S. 29. Guebelin, Edward *Precious Stones* (Stanford 1963)
S. 30. Hils, Karl *Creative Crafts* (Batsford 1966)
31. Hourd, Marjorie *The Education of the Poetic Spirit* (Heinemann 1949)
32. Hoyle, E. *The Teacher's Role* (Routledge & Kegan Paul 1968)
33. Hudson, Liam *Frames of Mind* (Methuen 1968)
34. Hudson, Liam *Contrary Imaginations* (Penguin 1968)
35. Hughes, A. G. & Hughes, E. H. *Learning and Teaching*, (Longmans 1960)
S. 36. Hurry, S. *The Microstructure of Cells* (Murray 1965)
37. Huxley, Aldous *Brave New World* (Penguin 1963)
38. Huyghe, R. *Larousse Encyclopaedia of Prehistoric and Ancient Art* (Paul Hamlyn 1962)
39. Johnson, Pauline *Creating with Paper* (Kaye 1960)
40. Kafka, Franz *The Trial* (Penguin 1966)
41. Kenny, J. B. *The Complete Book of Pottery Making* (Pitman 1950)
42. Laming, Annette *Lascaux* (Penguin 1959)
43. Langford, Glenn *Philosophy and Education* (Macmillan 1968)
44. Leach, Bernard *A Potter's Book* (Faber 1945)
45. Leach, Bernard *A Potter in Japan* (Faber 1967)
S. 46. Leigh-Pemberton, John *Ladybird: Heath and Woodland Birds* (Wills & Hepworth 1968)
47. Lovell, K. *An Introduction to Human Development* (Macmillan 1968)
48. Lowenfeld, Viktor *The Nature of Creative Activity* (Routledge 1952)
49. Lowenfeld, Viktor & Brittain, Lambert *Creative and Mental Growth* (Collier–Macmillan 1964)
50. MacKenzie, Norman *Dreams and Dreaming* (Aldus 1965)
51. Marshall, Sybil *An Experiment in Education* (Cambridge University Press 1963)
52. Meldgaard, J. *Eskimo Sculpture* (Methuen 1960)
53. Melzi, K. *Art in the Primary School* (Blackwell 1967)
54. Meyer, Hans *150 Techniques in Art* (Batsford 1965)
55. Mock, Ruth *Principles of Art Teaching* (University of London Press 1955)
56. Musgrave, P. W. *The School as an Organisation* (Macmillan 1968)
57. Nicol, W. D. *Terra Cotta* (Oxford University Press 1963)

58. O'Connor, Kathleen *Learning, An Introduction* (Macmillan 1968)

59. Oeser, O. A. (Ed.) *Teacher, Pupil and Task* (Tavistock 1966)

60. Orwell, George *Nineteen-Eighty-Four* (Penguin 1964)

61. Pluckrose, H. *Creative Arts and Crafts* (Oldbourne 1966)

S. 62. Portmann, Paul *Children's Games* (Stanford 1964)

S. 63. Postma, C. *Plant Marvels in Miniature* (Harrap 1960)

64. Read, Herbert *Education Through Art* (Faber 1958)

65. Read, Herbert *The Meaning of Art* (Penguin 1964)

S. 66. Reed, Olwen *Ladybird: Lighthouses, Lightships and Lifeboats* (Wills & Hepworth 1968)

67. Reilly, Paul 'A Speech to the Ravensbourne Assembly', January 1968 *N.S.A.E. pamphlet* (1968)

68. Rhodes, Daniel *Clay and Glazes for the Potter* (Pitman 1958)

69. Richardson, Marion *Art and the Child* (University of London Press 1948)

70. Rosenthal, E. *Pottery and Ceramics* (Penguin 1949)

71. Rottger, Ernst *Creative Clay Crafts* (Batsford 1962)

72. Rowland, Kurt *Looking and Seeing* (Ginn 1964)

73. Rump & Southgate 'Variables Affecting Aesthetic Appreciation in Relation to Age', *Br. J. Educ. Psychol.* (February 1967)

74. Ruscoe, William *A Manual for the Potter* (Tiranti 1959)

75. Sadler, J. E. & Gillett, A. N. *Training for Teaching* (Allen & Unwin 1962)

76. Satterly, David 'Perceptual, Representational and Conceptual Characteristics of Primary School Children (Research Notes)', *Br. J. Educ. Psychol.* (February 1968)

77. Savage, George *Pottery Through the Ages* (Penguin 1959)

S. 78. Scott, Nancy *Ladybird: Pond Life* (Wills & Hepworth 1966)

S. 79. Shaw, A. C. *Photomicrographs of the Flowering Plant* (Longmans 1964)

80. Ucko, J. & Rosenfeld, A. *Palaeolithic Cave Art* (Weidenfeld & Nicholson 1967)

S. 81. Unstead, R. J. *Looking at Ancient History* (Black 1959)

82. Wildenhain, Marguerite *Pottery, Form and Expression* (Reinhold 1962)

Glossary

ABSTRACTION. See page 19.

AN ABSTRACT. A conceptual image that holds no recognisable elements of the everyday world.

ARMATURE. The supporting skeleton of a piece of sculpture.

ARTEFACT. Something made by an artist.

BAT. A wooden modelling board, a plaster slab or a kiln shelf.

BISCUIT. Clay that has been fired once, without a glaze. See page 90.

COLLAGE. A design made by sticking objects onto a support. See pages 57–60.

CONCEPTUAL ART. Art that does not copy the real world.

DEVELOPMENTAL AGE. Indicates development, not years. See page 29.

EARTHENWARE. Pottery that is porous because it has not been fired above 1,150 °C.

EMPATHY. See pages 97–98 and 103–104.

ETHOS. The spirit that characterises a community or a system.

FIXATIVE. A quick-drying liquid that is sprayed on to charcoal or pastel to give limited protection from rubbing.

FORMATIVE. 'Of forming' or 'of formation'. Almost synonymous with 'creative', but the word often carries greater meaning because 'creative' has become debased. (It is even possible to have 'creative football' today.)

FRIT. See page 91.

GLAZE. See page 91.

GLOST. Glazed.

GRIFFON. A curved tool, very useful for work on leather-hard coil pots. From Tiranti.

GROG. See pages 72-73

HAPTIC. A haptic type of person attaches relatively great importance to his own body's sensations. He tends to experience the world subjectively. (49, chapter 9; 6; and 76.)

INTEGRATION. In education, this has come to mean a method in which barriers between subjects are crossed, and children learn by exploring and relating experiences.

LEATHER-HARD (cheese-hard) CLAY. See page 72.

MASK. A flat piece of cardboard, wood or metal that is cut to shape and placed on an artefact to shield it from spraying. Similar to a template.

MOBILE. See page 61-62.

MOSAIC. Strictly, a flat design made from small pieces of glass or stone known as *tesserae*. Broadly, any flat design made from relatively small objects, or by printing with small flat objects. See pages 60–61.

MUFFLE. See page 77.

NATURALISTIC. A naturalistic artist expresses the world very much as his eyes see it.

PYROMETER. An instrument that measures the temperature in a kiln.

RELIEF. A form of carving or modelling in which the subject-matter stands out from the ground plane.

SCHEMA. A single symbol used to represent many objects belonging to the same class. e.g. a child may have a regular schema for a human foot, whether it belongs to a girl or a man. Plural: schemata. (Not to be confused with Piaget's use of the word.) See page 29-30.

SLURRY. See page 81.

SLIP. See pages 87–88.

STONEWARE. Pottery that is fired over 1,200 °C, which makes it non-porous.

THEME TREE. A scheme of related ideas which grow out of each other and which are drawn up like a Family Tree. See page 114.

VISUAL. A visual type of person tends to 'live through his eyes'. He is an observer, who reacts to the world relatively objectively. (49, chapter 9; 6; and 76.)

VISUAL MUSIC BOX. See page 49.

Index